Comforting the Bereaved

Comforting the Bereaved

by

Warren W. Wiersbe

and

David W. Wiersbe

MOODY PRESS

CHICAGO

Library of Congress Cataloging-in-Publication Data

Wiersbe, Warren W.
  Comforting the bereaved.

  Bibliography: p.
  1. Church work with the bereaved.   2. Bereavement—
Religious aspects—Christianity.   3. Funeral service.
I. Wiersbe, David.   II. Title.
BV4330.W54   1985   259′.6   85-15499
ISBN 0-8024-5293-0 (pbk.0)

4 5 6 7 Printing/LC/Year 90 89 88

Printed in the United States of America

Contents

To that vast
and growing family of
people who have learned
that Jesus Christ can
heal the brokenhearted,
and who want to share
this comfort with others
who desperately need it.

Foreword

At the beginning of Jesus' ministry on earth He quoted — and said that He fulfilled — the prophecy of Isaiah 61:1: "The Spirit of the Lord is upon me, because he hath anointed me . . . to heal the brokenhearted" (Luke 4:18, KJV).

Hearts were broken then as hearts are broken now. And a prime sign that the Holy Spirit has anointed His servants (Jesus' undershepherds) today continues to be that we bring healing to the brokenhearted.

But it is not an easy part of ministry, especially for the young pastor who has experienced little personal loss. Most of us, professionals and lay persons alike, feel inadequate when confronted by a lifeless body and stunned family. What can we say to parents whose teenage son has taken his own life? whose daughter has died in a car accident? or whose child has been murdered? to the widow suddenly alone after forty years with her beloved companion?

And even before those questions can be answered, what do we know about grief? If we want to bear people's sorrows, we cannot be ignorant of the forms grief takes.

This book provides biblical, practical answers to those and many other questions that fill the mind confronted by overwhelming loss and grief.

For the pastor, suggestions about visitation, the funeral service (including texts and outlines), and long-term ministry to survivors greatly increase the book's value.

One of the most encouraging verses at a time of loss is Isaiah 63:9: "In all their affliction He was afflicted, and the angel of His presence saved them" (NASB).

Through understanding and applying this book, God's servant may become His angel (messenger) to those who are brokenhearted, saving them from despair.

Thank God a day is coming when tears shall cease and death shall be destroyed.

Joseph Bayly
Bartlett, Illinois

Preface

This book was written to help you minister God's comfort to those who are bereaved. Although much of it centers on pastoral ministry and was written with the pastor in mind, the concerned layperson can also benefit from the principles shared in these pages.

Alexander Maclaren, that great British preacher, said near the close of his ministry, "If I had to do it over, I would minister more to broken hearts."

Part 1 deals with death and grief from a biblical and psychological perspective. We believe that it is fundamental to our approach for you to understand this section. The busy pastor may be tempted to go immediately to part 3 and begin to use some of the message outlines; but we urge him to start with part 1.

Part 2 gives practical counsel to the minister on how to handle the grief situation and the funeral service. We believe that the layperson reading this book can benefit from this section as well.

It is impossible to deal with every kind of problem situation that death can bring to a family or a church, but in part 3 we have attempted to give some help concerning the ones that seem to occur most often.

What minister can ever forget the experience of conducting

that first funeral? In spite of his training, he probably felt help-less. It is our prayer that this book will help both pastor and people handle grief situations more effectively, and thus help to heal the brokenhearted.

The two of us bring to this book the experiences of nearly forty years of ministry. The examples given come from our own experience, but we have made sufficient alterations so that nobody will be embarrassed. If you think we have written about you, or somebody you know, it is probably because many sit-uations in life are a great deal alike. Also, whenever we write "We remember . . ." it means that the experience happened to one of us. It seemed ridiculous to write "I (WW)" or "I (DW)," because it really does not make any difference whose story it is! In fact, it is amazing how many almost identical experiences the two of us have had in our ministries.

We want to thank Jeaneane Linn who was able to read our rough copy and, with her typing skill, make a beautiful man-uscript out of it.

Part I

The Meaning of Comfort

Then Job answered and said,
"I have heard many such things:
miserable comforters are ye all!"
(Job 16:1-2)

Blessed be God, even the Father of our
Lord Jesus Christ, the Father of
mercies, and the God of all
comfort; who comforteth us in all
our tribulation, that we may be
able to comfort them which are in
any trouble, by the comfort wherewith
we ourselves are comforted of God.
(2 Corinthians 1:3-4)

Take this sorrow to thy heart, and
make it a part of thee, and it shall
nourish thee till thou art strong again.
(Longfellow, *Hyperion*)

1

Comforters Needed

Alice was a faithful Christian, devoted to God and her church. But when her fourteen-year-old daughter, Joanie, was killed by an automobile, all Alice could do was ask, "Why? Why?"

Her pastor arrived at the home and seemed threatened by her questions. "God is not to be questioned," he told her. "His ways are beyond our ways. The fact that you are questioning God shows that your faith is weak." Then he added, "I've noticed that your faith has *always* been weak."

The family was told not to cry, but to be happy because Joanie was with Jesus in heaven. At the funeral, the pastor gave a public invitation, and some of Joanie's friends responded. Later, the pastor used these "converts" as the reason God permitted Joanie's death. But the family had a hard time understanding why God had to work that way in order to save lost souls.

In the months that followed, Alice's Christian friends encouraged her to "be happy" and help to nurture the teenagers who had trusted the Lord at the funeral. Whenever she wanted to talk about Joanie or the accident, Alice was told to "turn it over to Jesus" and not mention it.

A year after the accident, Alice left the church and the faith. For three years she drifted, deeply hurt within and greatly confused about God and the Christian life. Her former church friends were sure she had never been a Christian at all. Then Alice began attending a church different from her former fellowship, but she still claimed she could not believe in the kind of God who deliberately caused accidents.

There are thousands of people like Alice in and out of our churches today, people who desperately want to trust God and have their deep wounds of sorrow healed. However, no one has yet accepted them as they are and shown them what God can do for them. Too many Christians, like Alice's own pastor, have pat answers for complex questions and simply do not understand the dynamics of grief. A broken heart is never healed by clichés like "Turn it over to Jesus!" or "Be happy that she's with the Lord in heaven." We wonder how many people have quietly left our evangelical churches, and perhaps even gone to non-Christian groups, simply because nobody shared with them the ministry of comfort.

The ministry of comfort is important in the local church and must be an important part of the church's ministry. To begin with, those who are bereaved need this ministry. Although there are times when grieving people want to be alone— and this is normal—there are also times when they must have the strength that comes from Christian friends standing near. But those who are standing near must know how to relate to their grieving friends, and these friends must not be threatened by their questions or their seeming rebellion against God.

Bob and Carol were in shock when their nineteen-year-old daughter was killed in an automobile accident. A beautiful young lady, Michele was the focus of their dreams and hopes. More than three hundred people attended the funeral, and the pastor lovingly emphasized God's grace and His ability to heal the brokenhearted. "The funeral seemed 'fuzzy' to us," the parents said later, "but having so many of our friends—and Michele's friends—around us, was a great source of strength." Nobody offered any explanations. They simply shared their love and tears and helped to fortify Bob and Carol when they needed it most.

Not only do the bereaved need the ministry of comfort, but the church family needs *to give* the ministry of comfort if it is to be a true fellowship of Christian people who minister to one another. "Weep with them that weep" is a vital ministry in the church (Rom. 12:15). Nowhere does the Bible say it is wrong for people to weep when loved ones are taken from them. Churches grow in unity and strength not only as they work and witness together, but also as they weep together. The fellowship of the broken heart is a large fellowship, and the initiation fee is very costly.

Everyone in the church loved Wilma. She had been the mainstay of the Sunday school for years. In fact, many of the adults were in her sixth-grade class when they were children. When Wilma came down with cancer, the church was shocked and saddened; and when she died, her homegoing left a gaping hole that nobody could easily fill.

The entire church family entered into the sorrow as well as into the ministry of comfort. The funeral message centered on the beauty of the Christian life and how it had been exemplified in Wilma. Those attending the funeral did not feel like spectators at a service: they were participants as they shared their sorrow as well as the joy of knowing that their friend was free from suffering and at home with the Lord. In the luncheon fellowship that followed, the friends openly mingled their laughter and tears as they remembered Wilma.

Later, a visitor said to the pastor, "I don't know if a funeral service can be called 'beautiful,' but if it can, then Wilma's sure qualified. It strengthened my own faith."

In today's busy world, it is easy for the church family to give only token respect to those in sorrow, or perhaps to ignore them completely. The larger the church, the more difficult it is for people to "weep with them that weep." It is much easier to send a sympathy card, contribute a few dollars to a floral piece, or make a quick visit to the funeral home the night before the service. Cards, flowers, and visits are important, and can be a meaningful part of the ministry of comfort; but broken hearts are not healed by proxy. Jesus did more than send a message to Mary and Martha: He traveled to Bethany, stood by the grave, and wept.

Not only during the initial time of shock and sorrow, but especially in the days and weeks afterward, the church family needs to show its love and support to those who are bereaved. It is that kind of ministry that draws people together, strength-

.ens faith and love, and helps to build the kind of unity that every church needs.

The ministry of comfort is noticed by unbelievers and those outside the church family. It is not necessary to turn a funeral service into an evangelistic meeting in order to witness to the lost; the very atmosphere of love, faith, and hope and the message from the Word can be used by the Spirit to convict and convert the lost. "Behold, how they love one another!" was the testimony of the ancient world as they saw those in the church family ministering to each other.

Later in this book, we will have more to say about the funeral as a witnessing time. But let it be said now that no amount of gospel preaching will make the impact that loving Christians can make as they minister to broken hearts. The message and the ministry must unite if the witness is to be authentic and effective.

The ministry of comfort is important to the bereaved, to the church family, and to the lost. But it is also important to the pastor. If his ministry of the Word is to be effective week after week, he must know what it means to minister to broken hearts. The pastor who is isolated and insulated, locked up in his study, is robbing himself and his people of some of the most enriching experiences of ministerial life. Quite frankly, we would not want to be members of a church whose pastor was so important, or so busy, that he did not have time to walk through the valley with us. To be sure, as churches grow, the pastor needs others to assist him because he can't do everything; but even those assistants will catch the spirit of the senior minister, whether he is concerned or indifferent.

Phillips Brooks said that the growing pastor must experience higher heights of joy and deeper depths of sorrow; and this is true. The promises of God take on new meaning when you read them through tears. Our church members quickly forget our sermons, but they remember our kindnesses, especially those dark hours when we were walking with them through the valley. Many pastors confess that they have learned more about the grace of God at an open casket than they ever learned from a profound theology book.

"Woe be to the shepherds of Israel that do feed themselves!" cried Ezekiel. "The diseased have ye not strengthened, neither have ye healed that which was sick, neither have ye bound up that which was broken" (Ezek. 34:2, 4). How strange it is that "busy ministers" have time for committee meetings and yet another seminar, but they have no time to weep with them that weep.

Perhaps the pastor never feels more inadequate than when he is ministering to the bereaved. Yet those may well be the times when God's Spirit is doing His greatest work. The minister who loves his people, walks with the Lord, and lives in the Word will know just what to say and do when these emergencies arise. Blessed is that congregation whose pastor is a true shepherd—who weeps with them that weep!

Alice's pastor was threatened by a situation he couldn't explain and a challenge he couldn't honestly face. Like Job's friends, he argued and accused, but he never really comforted. Instead of giving Alice and her family opportunity to be human—to weep, to ask painful questions, even to complain against God—he forced them to bury their true feeling *just so he could minister in a nonthreatening atmosphere*. Unfortunately, his ministry only drove the family farther from the Lord and the church, a result he conveniently attributed to lack of faith.

When the pastor ministers to the bereaved, he is putting his own Christian life to the test. He must be vulnerable or else he is not real. He must confess that there are questions he can't answer and feelings he may not want to face. Accustomed to talking, he must learn to be silent and listen. Accustomed to defending God and the Bible, he must lovingly relate to people who wonder if God really cares. The ground is level in the valley of the shadow of death, and the pastor cannot minister from some ecclesiastical eminence.

How often God's people have said to their shepherds, "You were such a help to us! We can never forget what you did!" But as the pastor reflected on "what he did," it seemed as though he had done very little. He visited the home, he listened, he showed that he understood their feelings, he pointed them to God, he related the Word to their needs, and he showed that he cared. There was nothing dramatic about his ministry, but God used it to heal broken hearts and bring peace to His troubled people.

Blessed is the Christian who understands the ministry of comfort!

What is the ministry of comfort?

Our English word *comfort* comes from two Latin words that together mean "with strength." The Holy Spirit of God is called "the Comforter" (John 14:16, 26; 15:26; 16:7) because He strengthens us and enables us to handle the challenges of life. The Greek word translated "comforter" simply means "one called alongside to help." It was used of a friend who represented you at court or who interceded for you in some specific way. The word could be translated "adviser," "counselor," or "advocate"; but perhaps the best translation would be "encourager." After all, to encourage somebody means to put courage into them, to give them heart.

It is unfortunate that our fine word "comfort" has taken on the meaning of protective sympathy. Often we seek to comfort people by trying to make life easy for them, by pampering them. But God comforts His children by putting within them the kind of courage and strength they need to face life honestly and live it faithfully. The worst thing we can do for suffering people is to pamper them and permit them to have their own way and escape pain. The best thing we can do for them is to be the kind of encouragers who help them face their trials honestly, work through their feelings, and see God give them His divine enablement.

We can minister comfort by our physical presence. "Just having you there was such a help to us!" is often what grieving people say. Job's three friends did him more good by coming to him and sitting with him in silence, then by trying to "counsel" him with their worn-out clichés and irrelevant personal experiences. It is wonderful to know that God is with us in the valley, but it is also wonderful to have our flesh-and-blood brothers and sisters in Christ standing with us.

We can minister comfort by what we say. The temptation is to say too much, to respond theologically to people's words and not to their feelings. Job's friends made that mistake. We must listen with the heart and respond to wounds, not words. "I loathe my own life," said Job; "I will give full vent to my complaint; I will speak in the bitterness of my soul" (10:1,

NASB*). His friends rejected his words, *but God accepted them*! God knew that Job's heart was filled with pain and that it was normal for him to "give full vent" to his sorrow.

We can minister comfort by sharing the Word of God. But we must not share God's truth the way a pharmacist mixes a prescription that he never takes. *We must share the Word that is meaningful to us.* This is why ministers must themselves suffer: they experience the grace of God and learn to lean on the promises of God, so that they in turn may minister to others. Martin Luther said that prayer, meditation, and suffering made a minister; and all three of these are tested when we seek to comfort the sorrowing.

We can minister comfort by praying, the kind of praying that gets through to God and opens the fountains of His grace. You don't minister true comfort by preaching a sermon over God's shoulder—especially to the lost who are present—but by leading people next to God's heart and showing them how sufficient He is for every need. In the house of sorrow, there is no room for theological lectures—even the keenest mind may be muddled by a broken heart. In the hour of sorrow, the prayer that comforts is the one that leads everybody into the presence of the loving Father where His peace can come to troubled hearts.

We can minister comfort by mobilizing the church family and instructing them how to encourage and not just sympathize. Each congregation needs a mature couple to be in charge of the ministry of comfort, to work alongside the pastor when death visits a home. This is no time for heroics. Rather, it is a time for an understanding, behind-the-scenes ministry that lets people know that the church cares.

When "Grandma" Hawkins died, her husband found himself wondering what to do next. The children lived in four different parts of the country and there were no other relatives nearby to give any assistance. The church family responded to the call and saw to it that the household routine was not upset, that people were at the airport to meet relatives flying in, and that the funeral director worked closely with the pastor and

* *New American Standard Bible.*

Comfort Committee in helping Mr. Hawkins with decisions that seemed to paralyze him. After the funeral, the committee prepared a lovely luncheon for all the relatives and guests; and in the weeks that followed, the members of the church family visited the home and assisted in whatever ways they could. When Mr. Hawkins elected to move to New York to be closer to his two sons, his biggest regret was leaving the church family behind.

The pastor can minister comfort by his preaching of the Word. This applies not only to the funeral message, but also to his week-by-week ministry from the pulpit and in the classroom. The pastor who publicly jokes about death, or who fails to apply the medicine of the Word to broken hearts week by week, is not going to have an easy time sharing the ministry of comfort.

Tom Seward took his own life near Christmas, leaving behind a shocked wife and three needy children. The church family rallied behind them and, in time, they worked through their grief and made a mature adjustment. A few months later, the church held a week of evangelistic meetings, to which Mrs. Seward invited some of her friends who had been impressed by the love shown to her by the church family. The evangelist, who should have known better, opened his first sermon by telling three jokes about death and funerals. Not only did Mrs. Seward and her children not attend the rest of the meetings, but her friends told her they would never go back to that church again.

Pastoral ministry is *built* week by week, but it is *tested* when the crises come along. In the regular course of his ministry, the pastor must build his people and help to prepare them for sorrow and death. He must seek to unite the congregation in a fellowship of caring. If the church is a large one, then there must be care groups within the congregation, so that nobody is ignored or isolated.

The time devoted to ministry to broken hearts is not *spent;* it is *invested.* Death is not an accident; it is an appointment (Heb. 9:27; Ps. 139:16). God not only appoints the time, but He also appoints the things He would like to see happen as a result of the event. The church family that learns to grieve together and encourage together will reap spiritual blessings that can come perhaps no other way.

In a general way, we have explained why the ministry of comfort is important to you and your church family. We will share the details later. First, we must consider what the Bible says about death, so that we have the right perspective as we seek to minister to those who have lost loved ones.

2

The Bible and Death

From Genesis 3 to Revelation 20, the Bible deals seriously with sin and its wages—death. In Romans 5:12-21, Paul explains the theology of death, pointing to Adam as the one whose disobedience brought sin and death into the world. He also points to Christ as the only Redeemer from sin and death.

The Bible uses the words *die, dead,* and *death* more than 1,300 times; and it records the deaths of scores of people, both good and evil. It also pictures death in a number of vivid ways, and a knowledge of these similes and metaphors can help the minister as he deals with death and seeks to comfort the bereaved.

OLD TESTAMENT PICTURES

1. *Sleep*—Deut. 31:16, Pss. 13:3 and 17:15; Jer. 51:39; Dan. 12:2. There is the repeated phrase "and he slept with his fathers," usually referring to the death of a king (1 Kings 2:10; 2 Kings 10:35; etc.) There is no suggestion that the soul sleeps. It is the body that rests in the dust (Dan. 12:2).

2. *Go to the eternal home*—Eccles. 12:5. The entire paragraph (vv. 1-7) is a graphic description of the decay of an old house, the body, and the release of the tenant (the human spirit) to go to dwell in an eternal home that will not decay.

3. *Grass cut down*—Pss. 90:5; 103:14-16; Isa. 40:7. This

image is quoted in James 1:10-11 and 1 Pet. 1:24.

4. *Water spilled*—2 Sam. 14:14. The idea here is that there is no return. Water spilled cannot be recovered again. Job gives the same idea in Job 14:10-12.

5. *An ember put out*—2 Sam. 14:7.

6. *Overwhelmed by waves*—2 Sam. 22:5; Ps. 42:7; Jonah 2:5.

7. *Darkness and shadows*—There are numerous references to this image. Here are a few: Job 3:5; 10:21; 12:22; 16:16; 24:17; Ps. 23:4; note the New Testament answer in 2 Tim. 1:10.

8. *A return to dust*—Gen. 3:19; Ps. 104:29; Eccles. 3:20 and 12:7.

9. *Going to one's fathers*—Gen. 15:15. The phrase "gathered to his people" is also used—Gen. 25:8 and 35:29.

10. *Giving up the ghost* (spirit)—Gen. 25:8 and 35:29; and see Eccles. 12:7.

The book of Job is especially rich in pictures of both the swiftness of life and the tragedy of death.

Life is swift like:

a weaver's shuttle—7:6

a breath—7:7

a passing cloud—7:9 (see James 4:14)

a swift messenger—9:25

a swift ship—9:26

a flying eagle—9:26

a withering flower—14:2

an intangible passing shadow—14:2

Some of the most vivid pictures of death are found in Job.

the crushing of a moth—4:19

the pulling up of a tent—4:21

the harvest sheaves cut down—5:26

the vanishing of a cloud—7:9

lying down in the dust—7:21; 21:26

sleep—7:21; 14:12

darkness—10:21-22

a tree chopped down—14:7-9

water spilled out—14:11-12

"the king of terrors"—18:14

a dream vanished—20:8-9

Job 18 is a dramatic presentation of the horrors of death. The death of the godless person is pictured as a light suddenly put out (5-6), a bird trapped (7-10, and he mentions six different kinds of traps), a criminal pursued (11-14), and a tree rooted up (15-21). The "king of terrors" cannot be avoided or appeased!

NEW TESTAMENT PICTURES

The New Testament borrows some of the Old Testament images, but it also adds a few new ones. Of course, the whole subject of death is, in the New Testament, taken out of the shadows and brought out into the light (2 Tim. 1:10).

1. *Sleep*—Matt. 9:24; John 11:11; Acts 7:60 and 13:36; 1 Cor. 15:6, 18, 51; 1 Thess. 4:13-18. Again, it is the body that sleeps; the spirit of the believer goes to be with the Lord.

2. *Absent from the body*—2 Cor. 5:8. The New Testament definition of death is the spirit leaving the body (James 2:26). The mortal body is our temporary house (see Eccles. 12:1-7), but we have a permanent glorified body awaiting in heaven (2 Cor. 5:1-4). Many theologians believe that there is some kind of an intermediate body between death and the resurrection.

3. *Departure*—Luke 2:29; Phil. 1:23; 2 Tim. 4:6. The Greek word means to take down a tent and move on; to set sail; to unyoke oxen; to solve a problem. These are certainly interesting insights into Christian death. When a believer dies, he is like a soldier; the battle is ended and he is moving to higher ground. He is like a sailor; the anchor is lifted, the storm is ended, and he sets sail for the heavenly shore. (Tennyson used this image in his poem "Crossing the Bar.") The believer's work is ended and his burdens are lifted, like oxen unyoked at the close of day. The many problems and mysteries of life are now solved as he enters the presence of the Lord.

4. *Exodus*—On the Mount of Transfiguration, Jesus spoke to Moses and Elijah about his exodus that He would accomplish at Jerusalem (Luke 9:31). He did not see His death as bondage, but as release! Just as God delivered Israel from Egypt by the blood of the Passover lambs, so the blood of the Lamb of God has delivered us from sin, death, Satan, and eternal judgment. The death of the Christian is a release, an exodus, and an entry

into a new and better country. Peter used the same image in
2 Pet. 1:14-15.

5. *Putting off a tent*—2 Pet. 1:14. This parallels the image
that Paul uses in 2 Cor. 5:1-4, and also relates to #3—*Departure*.

6. *Changing clothes*—1 Cor. 15:51-57.

7. *The planting of a seed*—1 Cor. 15:36-38 and 42-44, and
John 12:24. The believer's body is like a seed, and burial is the
planting of the seed. Christ is the resurrection "firstfruits" (1
Cor. 15:20, 23), giving the assurance that the entire harvest
belongs to God and that His people will one day be raised from
the dead.

8. *An enemy*—Heb. 2:14 with 1 Cor. 15:26.

9. *Rest*—Rev. 14:13.

10. *A king*—Rom. 5:14, 17. Every cemetery is proof that
death is reigning!

11. *Going home to the Father*—John 14:1-6. This ties in with
Paul's testimony "absent from the body, . . . present [at home]
with the Lord" (2 Cor. 5:8). Jesus pictured heaven as a loving
home where a special place is prepared for each of God's children. The Greek word translated "mansions" in the King James
Version simply means "abiding places." There is no suggestion
that the faithful Christian will have a "bigger mansion" than
the careless Christian. There is room for all, and all will rejoice
in the Savior's presence.

From a scientific and medical point of view, there is no
agreement on the definition of death. Doctors speak of at least
three levels of death: (1) *clinical death*, when the heart ceases
to beat and the respiration stops; (2) *brain death*, resulting in
a flat EEG (electro-encephalogram); (3) *cellular death*, when the
various parts of the body begin to cease functions and the
cells die.

The Council of the International Organization of Medical
Science determined in 1968 that at least five characteristics
must be present before the physician could declare the patient
dead: (1) no response to the environment; (2) no reflexes or
muscle tone; (3) no spontaneous breathing; (4) sudden decline
in blood pressure; and (5) a flat EEG. How long the medical
staff should monitor the patient and watch for these signs is a

matter of debate. Some say at least twenty-four hours; others opt for less time.

It is not the purpose of this book to enter into the complex problems that cluster around life-support systems, euthanasia, living wills, and so on. It would appear from Scripture that the issues of life and death are in the hands of God (Ps. 139:13-16). God has set the limits of life. We cannot go beyond those limits, but we can foolishly hasten our deaths. We believe that it is God's will that each person fulfill his or her years and accomplish the purposes God has in mind. Abraham died "an old man and full of years" (Gen. 25:8, NIV*), a phrase that suggests quality of life rather than quantity of time. His life was full. Godly men like Robert Murray McCheyne and David Brainerd died very young, yet they were still full of years in the same sense Abraham was.

Death is a divine judgment, executed upon our first parents because of their willful disobedience (Gen. 2:16-17; 3:3, 17-19). But it is also a divine provision of grace. If there were no death, corrupt sinners would live forever in a decaying environment, without hope. If there were no death, the Redeemer could not have come as the Last Adam to die for the sins of the world and open the doors to everlasting life.

We die individually, which shows the value of the individual to God. The person who wrote Psalm 116 was in danger of death, so he cried out to God for deliverance; and the Lord rescued him. Why? The answer is given in verse 15—"Precious in the sight of the Lord is the death of his saints." Death is not a cheap thing with God. It is not an accident; it is an appointment. He will not permit the death of one of His children to be treated with disdain or contempt. His children are precious, purchased by the precious blood of His Son; and He will not leave their homecoming to chance or fate.

But death is a mystery; we are not always sure when it happens. Anyone who has ever witnessed the death of a person understands what we mean when we say that mystery is present. Even in a busy institutional hospital, voices are hushed and reverence is shown to the dead body. Perhaps death is a

* New International Version.

mystery because *life* is a mystery. The only sure knowledge we have about death comes from the revelation in God's Word. In spite of the claims of the out-of-body people and the spiritists (and we are not suggesting that they are kin), nobody except Jesus Christ has ever died and come back to tell us anything about it.

One thing is sure: death draws a line and sets up a terminus for life. Unless Jesus Christ returns to take us to heaven first, we shall all die someday. Perhaps this solemn terminus helps to give value to life. "For we brought nothing into this world, and it is certain we can carry nothing out" (1 Tim. 6:7). We treasure our loved ones even more when we consider that we may not have them here very long. Each stage in life reminds us that we leave something behind as we move ahead in years, and that one day we shall make that final move. We are not implying that there would be no values in life were there no death, because God is the source of all values. We are suggesting that life becomes even more precious when we consider the reality of death.

Death also introduces uncertainty. "I know not the day of my death," said Isaac (Gen. 27:2); and practical James warns us, "Instead, you ought to say, 'If the Lord wills, we shall live and also do this or that' " (4:15, NASB). The rich farmer in our Lord's parable had a false sense of security because he ignored this warning (Luke 12:16-21). But uncertainty means that we must live by faith, so the reality of death ought to be an encouragement to people to hear God's truth and believe it.

Finally, death is final as far as this world is concerned. When our loved ones die, they can't return to us (2 Sam. 12:23). Death leaves an empty place in the home and the heart. It is like an amputation that really never heals. For the Christian, the finality of death only brightens the reality of heaven and makes the "blessed hope" that much more wonderful. For the unbeliever, this finality can lead either to hopeless despair or godless hedonism: "Let us eat and drink; for tomorrow we die" (1 Cor. 15:32).

Mankind should learn from death. What should we learn? Psalm 90 suggests that the reality of death ought to remind us of the sovereignty of God (v. 3), the frailty of man (vv. 4-6), the brevity of life and the need for wisdom in using our time (vv. 12-15), and the need to do God's work so that life will not be in vain (vv. 16-17).*

Death also teaches us the reality of sin and the necessity of being born again. Our time on earth is short; therefore, we must make the best use of our opportunities (Eccles. 9:10) and our possessions (Ps. 49:16-20; Luke 12:13-21). Death is the great leveler—all equally turn to dust (Ps. 49:7-10; Eccles. 2:14-18, and 6:6-10).

Isaiah 38 records the experience of King Hezekiah, the man who knew how long he would live. When confronted with the fact of death, he wept and prayed; and in grace, God gave Hezekiah fifteen more years of life. From this experience, Hezekiah certainly gained a new appreciation of life (vv. 15-16), a new confidence in prayer (vv. 2-3), and a new understanding of God's love (v. 17). It also resulted in his desire to serve the Lord, even though he committed at least one foolish blunder during the years God gave him (Isa. 39).

In verse 12, Hezekiah pictured death as the taking down of a tent, an image we have encountered before. But he also pictured it as a fabric cut off from the loom. "Like a weaver I have rolled up my life, and he has cut me off from the loom" (NIV). Life is a fabric that God weaves—only He can see the total pattern, and only He knows when the design is completed and the fabric ready to be cut off.

As we consider the biblical view of death, we need to recognize the fact that God's revelation of death and the afterlife was not given in its fullness until the coming of Jesus Christ to the earth. He "abolished death, and brought life and immortality to light through the gospel" (2 Tim. 1:10, NASB). It is a dangerous thing to build your doctrine of death on the basis of Old Testament Scriptures alone, as many of the cultists do. There are verses in the Psalms and Ecclesiastes that would seem to indicate a hopeless condition for all who die, believers and unbelievers alike. We must read these verses in the light of what Jesus did and taught and what the apostles explained.

---

* Psalm 90 was written by Moses and should probably be associated with the judgment of God on Israel at Kadesh-Barnea, Numbers 14. It should be interpreted in that light. In Psalm 91, Moses gives the other side of the picture.

However, whether you read about death in the Old Testament or the New Testament, you can be sure of this: the writers all take death seriously. Jesus never spoke lightly about death, nor did the apostles. The shadow of death is cast upon the longest life. Death is an enemy—the last enemy to be judged (1 Cor. 15:26; Rev. 20:14)—and we must respect this enemy, even though Jesus has defeated death for us.

3

The Grief Process

Just as it takes time for a broken bone to heal, so it takes time for a broken heart to heal; and the pain can be just as great, or greater. Each year in the United States some eight million persons experience the death of a close family member, and the loss of that loved one is very much like the loss of a limb. It is an emotional amputation, and it affects you deeply.

Doctors tell us that there is a definite relationship between illness and a grief badly managed. When the emotions do not heal properly, they affect the body and make the grieving person much more susceptible to certain illnesses. Loneliness and depression that are not handled in a mature way will certainly cause long-term problems that may not respond to medicine. Time by itself does not heal a broken heart. It all depends on what people do with time.

The pastor must be a part of the answer and not a part of the problem. He must understand what the grief process is and how he can minister effectively to those who sorrow. His task is not to shelter people from the pains of bereavement, nor to help them escape. Rather, his task is to help them draw upon the divine resources that God provides, so that they might accept their situation maturely, use it creatively, and finally emerge at the end of the valley better people than when they went into the valley.

Psychologists and counselors who have studied grief reaction tell us that there are certain stages to be expected in the experience of the bereaved person.

1. *Shock*. There is an emotional numbness when we hear that a loved one has died. This is a normal response triggered by the nervous system of the body. It is God's way of anesthetizing the person so that he or she might be able to face the reality of death and handle the difficulties to come. Of course, if this stage lasts too long, it is abnormal and will create problems.

2. *Strong emotion*. God made us to weep, and tears are always in order when there is a broken heart. The foolish counsel "Now, don't cry!" is based on both bad psychology and bad theology. Jesus wept, and so did the saints of God named in the Scriptures (Gen. 23:2; 50:1; 2 Sam. 18:33; Acts 8:2). *We are not told that it is wrong to sorrow. We are told that our sorrow should not be hopeless*, like the sorrow of the world (1 Thess. 4:13-18).

3. *Depression*. This is sometimes accompanied by a smothering feeling of loneliness. After all, the loss of a loved one (especially a parent or mate) forces a person to reorganize his or her whole life. Relationships are broken, and feelings of security are gone. The dedicated Christian must not think that he is above these normal expressions of grief. Sometimes there are even symptoms of physical problems. If the grief is not fully worked out, it could lead to *real* physical problems.

4. *Fear*. The bereaved person finds it difficult to think, to concentrate, and then becomes afraid and panicky. Life seems to be falling apart both on the outside and the inside. Sometimes well-meaning people misunderstand what the grief-stricken person is saying or doing, and this only leads to more fear and disorientation.

5. *Guilt*. A sorrowing person often has the tendency to blame himself or herself for the death of the loved one. This is especially true when it is death by suicide. Grief opens up old wounds and old memories. There is also the tendency to idealize the deceased person and see only the good points. This, in turn, exaggerates the bad points of the one grieving. "If only we had gone to another doctor!" is one characteristic response.

"He should have taken a different highway!" is another. This "if only" response is a normal expression of grief: the bereaved person takes all the blame. But there is more to it than that, as the next stage indicates.

6. *Anger.* Along with blaming himself or herself, the sorrowing person will also blame others, including the deceased. "Why did he have to leave me and the children now?" We remember old resentments and negative experiences, and these become a confusing part of our hurt feelings. We can do nothing about the loss of the loved one, and this frustration only creates more hostility. Sometimes people show this hostility by blaming God and even saying all kinds of blasphemous things. It is this feeling of guilt and anger that helps to cause some of the family problems that often cluster about funerals. Death not only creates problems, but it also *reveals* them.

7. *Apathy.* It seems strange that hostility can be replaced by apathy, but this is often the case. "Nobody understands how I feel!" and, since they do not, there is no sense saying or doing anything. "Life is not worth living." The bereaved person finds it painful to relate to real life and wants to withdraw into his or her own shell and be left alone. Certainly it is normal for a hurting person to want to be left alone; but if this withdrawal continues too long, it becomes dangerous.

8. *Adjustment.* Slowly the person learns to accept the loss, rearrange his or her life, and come to grips with reality. This does not mean the total absence of grief, loneliness, or bewilderment; but it does mean that the bereaved person recognizes what is happening and is able to cope with it. People die, but relationships never die; and each of us must struggle to adjust to the new relationship with the one who has passed away. There are definite signs when this adjustment is taking place: the bereaved person can openly and easily talk about the dead loved one, and, in time, even laugh about things that happened in the past. The person no longer gives vent to hostility but, instead, seeks for ways to minister to others when they suffer loss.

We must not assume that every person will go through all of these eight stages, or that the stages will necessarily be in this order. But if we are to comfort others in a creative way, we must learn to recognize these symptoms and accept them. We must also realize that no amount of preaching will eliminate hostility and guilt. The sorrowing person must learn to face these feelings personally and deal with them in his or her own time.

Often the pastor finds himself serving as a referee at a family funeral feud, and he wonders what to do. The first thing he should do is realize that such expressions of anger are perfectly normal, even though they may be unpleasant. He must never take sides. All he can do is listen with his heart and pay attention to *feelings*, not to words. He must not assume the posture of Job's comforters and try to argue people into a right relationship with God and each other. It is unfortunate that Job's three friends listened to Job's *words* and not his *feelings*.

It takes time for grief to heal; and, while the process is going on, the sorrowing person needs acceptance and assurance. "Grief has its time," said Samuel Johnson. "While grief is fresh, every attempt to divert only irritates. You must wait til grief be *digested*."

That is why post-funeral ministry is so important. As we relate to the bereaved person, we help to create that necessary atmosphere of acceptance and assurance. Our mature responses help the person clarify his or her own feelings, and this helps the adjustment to take place.

Should the pastor *never* interfere and confront the grieving person? He must interfere when the person's decisions will permanently do damage. During the "guilt" stage of mourning, the person may want to atone for past sins against the deceased by spending a great deal of money on an elaborate funeral or gravemarker. We recall one lady of modest means who was ready to spend her entire life-savings on a casket. It was her way of atoning for the "sin" of not being at the hospital when her husband died. Fortunately, the wise funeral director understood the situation and helped to solve the problem.

These eight stages are only guidelines; do not force them into every grief situation. You are there to comfort, not to analyze and explain. Understanding them, however, will help you to assess the situation better and not be too shocked at what you see or hear.

You also want to be aware of what the psychologists call

"distorted reactions" in times of grief. People who repress their grief ("Mother is being so strong and brave!"), or who delay it, often give evidence of abnormal behavior that may require professional care. Grieving people who become hyperactive (shopping, cleaning, even painting the house) are sometimes trying to avoid facing reality. Their activities are only distractions; and, when the outburst of energy subsides, they have *less* strength with which to face their real situation.

In fact, most of the normal stages of bereavement can become abnormal if taken to excess. Abnormal guilt could lead to threats of suicide, and anger taken to extremes could result in lack of self-control and open hostility against God, family, and life itself. If apathy is taken too far, it becomes isolation, the kind of physical and emotional withdrawal that hinders normal grief therapy. God has ordained that we cannot heal a broken heart by ourselves; we need the presence of others.

How do we encourage the normal healing of grief? The most important ministry we can have is that of *listening*. What the heart feels must be expressed through the lips. Emotions expressed become medicines that heal; emotions repressed become poisons that kill. Blessed is that congregation that has a pastor who knows how to keep his mouth shut and his ears open to the *feelings* expressed by the words spoken.

This is not to suggest that the comforter is passively silent. Real listening is hard work and demands active participation of both mind and heart. The compassionate pastor responds to the person's feelings, reflecting verbally his interpretation of what the person is trying to say. Sometimes the person will say nothing, and the sensitive pastor accepts that silence and does not violate it.

What are we watching for as we listen? Evidences that the person is coming to grips with reality and drawing upon the spiritual resources available through Jesus Christ. Is he or she able to accept the fact of the death of the loved one? Are the memories of the deceased gradually becoming positive and creative rather than negative and destructive? The ability to talk about the deceased is important to normal grief therapy.

Another good sign is the person's ability to understand the past and plan for the future. He or she starts to sort things out and make mature decisions. Often during the time of official mourning, others are making decisions and protecting the bereaved from problems; but eventually that emotional honor guard has to be removed and the bereaved must reenter the world of painful realities.

The ability to laugh is another good sign, for a sense of humor usually indicates a sense of perspective. The ability to laugh at ourselves—even our stupid blunders—usually announces that we are facing reality and do not feel threatened by it.

When the bereaved person stops condemning himself or herself, it is an indication that healing is taking place; also when he stops indulging in self-pity.

Not everybody will adjust at the same time or in the same way. Our hurts are personal, and so are our healings. Wise is the pastor who allows people to be themselves and who accepts them as they are.

Some pastors have learned that bereaved people often "bottom out" about six to eight weeks after the funeral. By that time most of the post-funeral activity is over, decisions have been made, friends are not calling as frequently (if at all), and circumstances have forced the sorrowing people to get back into the stream of life. The compassionate pastor will keep regular contact with his hurting people and will establish the kind of growing relationship that invites them to share their needs. He will not be surprised if he hears that the grieving people have experienced a new wave of sorrow and pain. He will be there to help them face it and grow.

"You never get over it," said one grieving father whose son was killed in an auto accident, "but you do get through it."

When an entire family is touched by grief, each member will respond in a different way. In fact, some members may not seem to respond at all; but they are probably hiding their grief just to make it easier for the rest of the family, especially the children. We hurt individually, but we can grieve together; and this needs to be encouraged. Grief expressed can build bridges, but buried grief only builds walls. A father who represses his feelings may "fall apart" weeks later when his family needs him the most. Being able to cry together is a necessary part of therapy, and it brings healing.

When death invades a family, it can reveal both the strengths and weaknesses of that home. Sibling rivalry is sometimes discovered in a statement like "Dad always liked you best anyway!" A grieving wife may complain about her deceased husband's inability to provide for the family or even plan for the future. Then she will feel guilty because she let the skeleton out of the closet. There is a saying among lawyers, "Where there's a will—there are relatives!" The love of money is indeed the root of all kinds of evil, and covetousness is no respecter of death. Although the pastor probably should not get involved in family financial affairs, he must be alert to spiritual and emotional problems that can bring additional sorrow and trials.

"Grief is the agony of an instance," said Benjamin Disraeli, "the indulgence of grief, the blunder of a life."

Our task as Christian comforters is to help people face grief honestly and courageously and use their painful experience of sorrow as a means of growth. Fortunately, we are not left to our own human resources. We have divine resources to share with others because of what Jesus Christ has done for us.

God can heal the brokenhearted—if all the pieces are given to Him.

4

Pastoral Resources

Of himself, the pastor has nothing that can heal a broken heart. "Our sufficiency is of God" (2 Cor. 3:5). No matter how many funerals he has conducted, or bereaved persons he has tried to encourage, the minister must never depend on his experience or his expertise. Nor should he give the impression, "I've been through this many times! Just see what I can do!"

We read somewhere that the average American experiences a death in the family once every twenty years. The pastor, on the other hand, confronts sickness and death regularly, as a part of his work; and he must be careful not to become too professional. One pastor we know conducted fifty-six funerals during the first fifty-four months of his ministry.

The very presence of the pastor is a source of comfort and assurance to those who are bereaved. If he is a man of God, known to love his people, then he will be welcomed into the house of mourning, and his words will carry weight. He must ask the Lord to help him identify with the mourners and be sincere in what he says. As he ministers to the sorrowing, he must draw upon the spiritual resources that can come only from the throne of grace.

To begin with, he must be careful in what he says and how he says it. One minister was asked by the son of the deceased, "Well, pastor, how are you?" It was a routine question, but the minister replied, "I'm very tired." He realized too late that the family had been at the hospital all night, while he had been comfortably at home in bed. However, that kind of gauche reply can be forgiven; what cannot be forgiven is the lighthearted banter and joking of the pastor who thinks that everybody needs a good laugh.

The minister must not adopt the role of resident theologian and try to explain everything. People may ask him theological questions, but behind those questions is usually a much deeper problem of faith that the person is wrestling with. Furthermore, once the trauma of death is over, and the healing begins, many of these intellectual questions have a way of solving themselves. Even if we could give adequate explanations, we know that explanations never heal a broken heart, no matter how they may satisfy the mind.

Our best resource is the Word of God. The pastor must so know his Bible that he will have God's promises and assurances available when they are most needed. Just about everybody knows Psalm 23 and John 14:1-6, but there are other Scriptures that speak to our needs and uplift us in the hour of sorrow. The verses need not be about death or grief; they may simply focus on the presence of God, His compassion and concern for our needs. As the minister goes to the house of mourning, he should ask the Spirit to bring to mind the Scriptures that will be needed.

Here are a few that we have found helpful and meaningful:

> Psalm 16:11—God's guidance and presence
> Psalm 18:30—He makes no mistakes
> Psalm 20:1-2—God sends us help
> Psalm 22:24—God is sensitive to our needs
> Psalm 27:5—God's gracious protection
> Psalm 30:5—Joy in the morning
> Psalm 34:17-19—God hears and delivers
> Psalm 46—Our refuge and strength
> Psalm 48:14—Our guide even to death
> Psalm 55:22—Give God your burden
> Psalm 73:23-25—God is all we need
> Psalm 84:11-12—Grace and glory!
> Psalm 91:1-2—The shadow of the Almighty

Isaiah 40:28-31—Power to the faint
Isaiah 41:10—God is with you
Isaiah 43:1-2—Through fire and water
Jeremiah 29:11—God's thoughts of peace
Lamentations 3:22-26—God's faithfulness
Matthew 11:28-30—The promise of rest
John 10:27-29—His sheep are safe
John 11:25-26—The resurrection and the life
John 14:27—The gift of peace
John 16:22—Joy in the midst of sorrow
John 17:24—Jesus prays that we will be in heaven
Romans 8:28, 35-39—God's all-conquering love
1 Corinthians 15:55, 57-58—Victory over death
2 Corinthians 1:3-4—The God of all comfort
2 Corinthians 4:16-18—Weighing our sorrows
2 Corinthians 5:1-8—Present with the Lord
2 Corinthians 12:9—God's sufficient grace
Philippians 4:6-7, 13—God is adequate
1 Thessalonians 4:13-18—Promise of reunion
Hebrews 2:9—Jesus tasted death for us
Hebrews 4:15-16—The throne of grace
Hebrews 11:13—Strangers and pilgrims
1 Peter 1:3-5—Kept for glory
1 Peter 5:10—Grace, suffering, and glory
1 John 3:1-2—We are God's children
Revelation 21:1-5—All things new!

Many times we have seen the Word of God quiet hearts in a wonderful way. The sensitive pastor will use Scripture as medicine to heal (Ps. 107:20) and as light to overcome the darkness. He will trust the Spirit of God to apply the Word to hearts in His own way. The beautiful thing about Scripture is that it meets the need without violating the personality. A promise from God will calm the heart and yet will permit the person to weep and express normal grief. "Joy in the midst of sorrow" is often the believer's experience.

Even if the pastor carries a pocket New Testament or Bible, he may want to use one of the Bibles in the home. In his praying, he may quote the Scriptures; but it is best to read from the open Bible, even if he knows all the passages by heart. The focus of attention should be on what God is saying and not on the pastor's wonderful memory.

Our second resource is prayer, and the growing pastor ought to be able to lead grieving people to the throne of grace in a way that is suited to their needs and situation. The prayer must not be a sermon over God's shoulder, or an abbreviated counseling session. It must be worship at its best, the man of God gathering the feelings and needs of his people together and presenting them at the throne of grace. He must speak for the brokenhearted to the God who heals broken hearts.

George MacDonald wrote, "Nothing is so deadening to the divine as an habitual dealing with the outsides of holy things." When a man visits several homes or hospitals each day, and prays for many people, he may find himself unconsciously falling into a set pattern that robs his prayers of reality and life. Nothing but a vital relationship with the Lord and a growing sensitivity to spiritual truth can rescue the minister from that kind of routine religion. He must draw constantly from the hidden springs of the Spirit and depend on the Lord to give him utterance when needed.

In his prayer at the home, as well as at the funeral, the pastor should identify the feelings of the people, and then relate those feelings to the God of all grace.

> Father, we come today as confused and brokenhearted children. We don't understand, but we do trust You and know that You are still in control. We cannot change the past, but we do need strength for today and hope for the future. We know you see our sorrow, and we remember that Jesus wept. We're thankful that He is here with us to heal the brokenhearted. You know the feeling of shock that we have experienced, and you have promised to meet our need.

The pastor has accomplished several things in this prayer so far: (1) he has verbalized how people feel and has shown that he understands; (2) he has made it clear that God expects us to grieve, that tears are normal; (3) he has affirmed the presence of the Lord; and (4) he has opened the way for God to graciously meet their needs. He will express those needs as he continues to pray.

How personal should the prayer be? As personal as the pastor is with the people involved. But if he begins to name people individually, he may forget somebody; and hearts are extremely sensitive during times of sorrow. The important thing is not that everybody be named, but that the feelings and needs of the people be expressed and given to the Lord. The pastor who has been with the family for many years may be able to say things that a newer and younger minister might not be able to say.

There are times when the prayer should be ended with a benediction, as though the minister were concluding a worship service. The priestly benediction from Numbers 6:24-26 is especially appropriate for the house of sorrow; but if he uses it in the home, the pastor may not want to repeat it at the funeral or the graveside. The Hebrews 13:20-21 benediction is a bit long for the home and probably ought to be used in a more formal worship setting. Romans 15:13 is suitable, as are 2 Corinthians 13:14; 2 Thessalonians 3:16; 1 Peter 5:10; and Jude 2.

The growing minister will want to keep abreast of the work being done in grief counseling. If seminars are available in that field, he ought to avail himself of them. Although he may not agree with some of the ideas they present, he can certainly learn from men and women who specialize in the psychology of bereavement.

Another resource is the local fellowship of bereaved people, which may function under any number of different names: "Bereaved Parents," "Compassionate Friends," "Charlie Brown's Kids" (for children who have lost a parent or parents). Sometimes there is a special group for parents who have had a child commit suicide. The local family service agency should be able to supply information.

The local pastor should get acquainted with these groups as the guest of someone who is a member. And he had better be prepared for some negative reactions when the members discover he is a minister! Sad to say, many people in these groups have been deeply hurt by ministers who perhaps meant well but were insensitive in their ministry to them. The honest pastor can learn a great deal from hurting people in this kind of a fellowship, and perhaps he might be able to help them.

Part 2

Sharing Comfort

Comfort ye, comfort ye my people,
saith your God

(Isaiah 40:1)

Sympathy is a supporting atmosphere,
and in it we unfold easily and well.

(Ralph Waldo Emerson)

Unto a broken heart
No other one may go,
Without the high prerogative
Itself hath suffered, too.

(Emily Dickinson)

Jesus wept.

(John 11:35)

5
The Pastoral Visit

When death occurs, the pastor is usually notified and asked to join the family, whether at the hospital or at home. He should go as soon as possible, always taking into consideration the convenience of the family. It is not a question of "Shall I come?" but "When would you like me to come?" Unless he is involved in pastoral ministry that simply cannot be interrupted, the minister should hasten to the house of mourning, even if circumstances do not permit him to make a long visit.

We believe that most pastors respond in this way; but we must confess that we have heard about men who have been careless, and even cruel, in their handling of grief situations. One pastor made no visit to the home at all, except on the day of the funeral. He showed up at the front door and asked very professionally, "Where is the obituary?" While at the home he read no Scripture, offered no prayer, even extended no sympathy. The family never quite got over it.

Even if a family member says, "Oh, pastor, it isn't necessary for you to come!" the compassionate shepherd will respond with, "Unless you find it inconvenient, I would like to come anyway." If people are accustomed to their pastor's caring ministry, they will expect him to come.

The presence of their pastor reminds the family of God's presence and concern for them in their time of grief. It also reassures the family that they are not alone, that the church family is standing with them and praying for them. The pastor wins the right to be heard in public when he shares his concern in private.

Death is always an intruder, and a funeral is always an interruption. The pastor must be willing to change his own schedule so that he might minister to those in need. But he should remember that the loved ones are going through a time of severe disruption and irreversible change. He merely has to rearrange his schedule; they must rearrange their lives.

Bear in mind that every situation is different and that no two families—or persons—respond the same way to the death of a loved one. And we may be surprised to find that the ones we thought had a deep faith show the least amount of trust in the Lord. Make no permanent evaluations on the basis of the crisis situation. Be kind to everyone and do not be fooled by appearances.

Listening with compassion is the chief priority. Whether the death was sudden and unexpected or at the end of a painful time of suffering, the people involved will ask questions and express intense emotions—shock, grief, bewilderment, even hostility and anger. The minister must help to create an atmosphere of openness and acceptance in which people may feel free to be themselves and express themselves. The pastor himself may become the target for some hostility, and he must not react in kind. People who hurt sometimes want to blame God, so they blame God's servant instead.

This first visit is not the time for profound theological discussions. There will be time for questions and discussions later. Nor is it a time for clichés and trite answers, both of which clearly announce that the pastor does not really care but is simply making a professional visit. Sometimes the best thing to do is just to sit and listen and say nothing, and there is nothing wrong with sincere tears. The longer a minister shepherds the flock, the more painful are the departures; and he might as well admit it.

During the visit, the pastor can gain some helpful insights into the dynamics of the family grief situation; and these insights can help him in planning the funeral message and the post-funeral ministry.

For one thing, family relationships will be on display. Which family members are closest to each other? Which ones do not seem to get along well together? Are the family members trying to help each other, or are they simply hovering and waiting to pounce on the inheritance? Are there evidences of guilt? Is there a relative who refuses to weep? ("I'll cry later.") Or is there someone who cannot stop crying?

The careful pastor will note these signals but not try to solve the problems immediately. There will be time after the funeral for him to visit and chat with the people and help them face and solve their problems.

Since the average American family experiences a death only once every twenty years, this will be a whole new experience for many of the relatives. They may not know that it is normal to cry, to feel helpless, to want to fight back at something or someone. The men in particular may not feel comfortable shedding tears. They need to be assured that sometimes the strongest thing a man can do is weep. After all, *Jesus wept*.

If the minister himself has experienced deep grief, then he will know something of how the loved ones feel. He will accept their feelings and try to interpret them to the mourners, without giving a lecture on psychology or grief therapy. He will not say, "Yes, I know just how you feel." People experiencing shock and grief are quite sure nobody has ever gone through what they are enduring, and saying "I know how you feel," is like waving a red flag.

Reassurance is the major goal. They need to know that their feelings are normal, they have not lost control of life; and in due time, everything will settle down and be balanced once again. They need to be encouraged to live a day at a time and not to make too many decisions before they are really ready to act.

During the visit, the minister will probably hear a good deal of reminiscing about the deceased loved one. Some memories will even prompt laughter, and somebody may express the idea that laughter is wrong at a time like that. Not so. Both laughter and tears help us keep in touch with reality.

The pastor must respect the privacy of the family. His role is to be supportive and not to make official decisions for them.

Nor should he take advantage of the situation and exploit them. It is always right to bear witness to Christ and the gospel, but it is not ethical or loving to force a "salvation decision" on a person at a time of weakness and emotional pressure.

The minister should try to get as much information as he can concerning the funeral plans: the time and place of the service, plans for visitation, Scriptures and music desired, others who may share the service, the reading of the obituary, and the plans for burial, are the most important items. After the visit in the home, the pastor should contact the funeral director and work out the details. He should also see to it that the word is spread throughout the congregation so that the members can begin to rally their support and help for the grieving family.

Official information about the deceased is available from the funeral director and the church office, if the deceased was a member of the Sunday school or church. The official obituary published in the newspaper is usually correct, but don't take any chances. Check it out with the family or the funeral director. Of course, you will want to add personal matters that relate to the church and your own contact with the deceased.

If the service is to be held in the funeral home, then the funeral director will worry about the sound system, the organist (unless there is a special request from the family), and the other factors involved. But if the service is to be at the church, you must be sure that somebody gets the correct information and has everything ready. The funeral director should know whom to contact (trustee, custodian, deacon, pastor) in case problems should arise.

Sometimes the planning of a funeral service creates (or reveals) problems in the family. As we have noted, grief has a way of opening up old wounds and also of exaggerating trivial matters. We have seen mature adults fiercely arguing over what hymn the deceased loved the most! The loving pastor is careful not to allow the conversation to move into dangerous areas; and, if it does, he simply says, "Well, we still have time to make a decision. Let's just leave it for now." Then, later, he consults the "senior" family member and reaches some kind of happy compromise.

The minister must not get so involved in gathering information that he fails to perceive and evaluate the atmosphere of the home and the responses of the mourners. He certainly wants to have some personal "feel" for the situation; otherwise, his ministry in the home and at the funeral could be completely off-target. Is there resentment against the deceased, or bitterness? Is there genuine sorrow or abnormal sorrow that may suggest feelings of guilt? Is the family united in its faith, or is there a divided home? (Even though you may know the family, you will likely meet relatives you have never met before.) How are the younger members of the family responding? Is the situation in the home tense or relaxed? Are the right decisions being made by the right people?

We are not suggesting that the pastor appoint himself as either funeral director or referee. But as the spiritual guide for the family, he must be alert to what is going on. It will help him in his planning and his praying, and it may give him some clues for his post-funeral ministry to the bereaved.

The pastor certainly must respect whatever boundaries are laid down by the family. He will do nothing to compromise his testimony, of course; but he will, as much as possible, cooperate with all who are involved to make certain that the wishes of the deceased and his loved ones are carried out. Sometimes it takes a great deal of love, tact, and patience to handle some matters; but the minister who loves his people can usually "speak the truth in love" and avoid embarrassing and unbiblical pitfalls.

One of the best ways for the pastor to keep himself out of most embarrassing situations is to let people know in advance what his convictions are about certain funeral customs. He can discuss these matters with his church leaders and let the information filter down through the congregation. It does not take long for the word to get out. One minister of music let it be known that there were some songs he simply would not permit to be used at a public funeral service, and the church respected his desires.

Most church members expect the pastor to lead them in a brief time of worship whenever he visits the home, and this kind of ministry is especially needed at the hour of sorrow. He need not read a long portion of Scripture, but he ought to focus the hearts of the bereaved on the unchanging promises of the Word of God. He might even invite the family to read or recite some familiar Scripture with him, perhaps John 14:1-6 or Psalm 23. His prayer should center on the living, not the dead.

The most important thing about this first visit is that it be welcomed. If the minister feels out of place, he should offer to pray and then leave as quickly and unobtrusively as possible. There will be another day and another opportunity.

If the pastor can bring his wife along on the visit, so much the better.

Finally, he should be careful to write down the facts he will need to prepare his funeral message and other public ministry. If he depends on his memory, he will be embarrassed. He should note the songs to be used, the Scriptures, the participants, and so on, and check them with the family before he goes. There may be changes the next day, but at least he will know where he is going.

The wise minister begins his serious preparation as soon as he leaves the home. He lifts his heart to God in prayer for divine insight and direction. If the death has been labeled "tragic"—a murder or suicide, or an accident—then he will especially need God's wisdom as he prepares the message and plans the service. James 1:5 is still in the Bible!

This is a good place to deal with a special problem that any pastor can face: the deceased is a stranger to you and you know little or nothing about him. That can occur when you are new in the church, or when the funeral director phones and asks you to conduct the funeral for someone outside your church. What do you do?

You begin, of course, with the family. But try not to ask too many questions, because there are other ways to get information. "Tell me about this picture on the mantle" will get you more facts about the family than if you asked, "Now, what was your husband's family like?" Often when there is a death in the family, out come the photo albums and memorabilia; and this gives the uninstructed pastor opportunity to get much of the information he needs.

Another suggestion is to chat with family members and say, "You knew Mr. Hardy a long time. You must have some interesting memories." Mingling with the family when they arrive at the funeral home for visitation, the pastor can learn a great deal about both the deceased and the family. We have asked people, "What do you remember most about ——" (your uncle, grandfather, etc.)? Their answers can give you insights that will help you plan the message and the service better.

But don't believe everything you hear! We recall one funeral where the minister emphasized the "beauty of the Lord" because he was told that the deceased loved flowers very much. He discovered that the man not only ignored flowers but was allergic to them! Alas, the pastor got his misinformation from a neighbor who was only making polite conversation at the funeral home.

Fortunately, the days of prolonged wakes are over, and grieving people need not endure nearly a week of emotional stress as they sit with the body and meet their friends. The efficient funeral director can usually have everything in readiness within a day or two of the death; and now, in most places, there is but one evening of visitation, and the funeral is held the next day.

The caring pastor will try to be at the funeral home before the family arrives for that first viewing. He should, with the funeral director, meet them at the door, and then have prayer with them before they go into the chapel. Even if the casket is to be closed, there is something traumatic about entering a funeral home to pay respects to a loved one who has died. Having the shepherd there helps to assure the sheep.

Even if the deceased and the family are strangers to him, the pastor ought to be there in advance. This is a splendid time to get acquainted, bear witness to the gospel, and show the bereaved that you are compassionate and concerned. The alert shepherd can rescue many a lost sheep through funeral ministry, if he is present when people need him the most.

This visit need not be a long one. As other friends and relatives of the deceased start to come in, the pastor can conveniently excuse himself. However, if the family wants him to remain to meet special people, he should stay as long as possible. The more people he meets personally, the easier it will be to speak to them at the funeral service. He should not think that this time is wasted; it is wisely invested, and it can bear rich dividends as he ministers to the family in weeks to come.

Ten Commandments for Comforters

1. Go to those who arc bereaved as soon as possible, even if it is inconvenient for you.

2. Be swift to hear, slow to speak, and slow to react to words and feelings that may appear "un-Christian."

3. Do not try to explain everything.

4. Share the promises of God.

5. Avoid saying, "I know just how you feel." Nobody will believe you, and the statement accomplishes nothing.

6. Words often fail, so express yourself through a loving hug, a handshake, even a simple touch. Just being there is a ministry.

7. Do not be afraid to "weep with those who weep."

8. Remember that grieving is a difficult process that takes time. Be patient with those who mourn and try not to say, "Aren't you over it yet?"

9. Visit regularly during the weeks after the funeral.

10. Keep confidence. Don't turn the experience into a sermon illustration, unless the family gives you permission.

6

Do We Need Funerals?

In his poem "A Wish," published in 1867, Matthew Arnold wrote:

> Spare me the whispering crowded room,
> The friends who come and gape and go,
> The ceremonious air of gloom—
> All, which makes death a hideous show.

A cynic might well define a funeral as an event that enriches the undertaker, tires the preacher, snarls the traffic, entertains the onlookers, and only adds to the grief of the mourners who have to pay the bill both financially and emotionally. But Christians are not cynics; we must look at the funeral from a biblical and pastoral perspective.

In the mid-sixties, it was popular to question both the necessity for funerals and the integrity of those in the mortuary profession. Jessica Mitford's *The American Way of Death* (Simon and Schuster, 1963) and Ruth Mulvey Harmer's *The High Cost of Dying* (Crowell-Collier, 1963) both attempted to "expose" the paganism and excessive costs of the American funeral. Although the books did bring to light some of the abuses in the funeral industry, neither one seemed to affect our burial customs very much.

In 1935, the average cost of an adult funeral was about $350. Twenty-five years later, it was over $1,000. Today, the average cost for a funeral is about $1,800. It jumped 31 percent from 1977 to 1982, which was less than inflation. However, the prices went up on many other services; and funeral directors have to deal with rising costs just as the rest of us do.

Certainly a bereaved family has to consider the economics of the situation. Although we have not personally met any funeral directors who seemed to want to exploit grieving people, there are shysters in every profession; and we must watch out for them. But to conclude that there shall be *no funerals* simply because they cost too much is to draw a foolish conclusion from a dubious premise. The local funeral director can arrange a funeral to fit almost every budget; and, if a person is really exercised over this matter, he can arrange for a prepaid funeral.

Is there a need for a funeral service? Yes, *provided it is the right kind*. We can do without the kind of funeral that Matthew Arnold described in his poem.

What, then, are the purposes of the funeral?

For the Christian, the first purpose is to *glorify God*. "Whether, then, you eat or drink or whatever you do, do all to the glory of God" (1 Cor. 10:31, NASB). Unless the funeral service is seen as an act of Christian worship, and is planned with that in mind, it will lack the depth of meaning and ministry that sets it apart from a mere humanistic service. After all, God is the author of life, and our times are in His hands (Ps. 31:15). Jesus Christ alone holds the keys of death (Rev. 1:18).

It is difficult for the unbeliever to understand how the Christian can worship God even in the midst of pain and sorrow. Yet, by the grace of God, it is possible. We can say with Job, "The Lord gave and the Lord has taken away; may the name of the Lord be praised" (Job 1:21, NIV); and, with Jesus in the garden, we can pray, "Yet not as I will, but as you will" (Matt. 26:39, NIV).

If it is to be a worship service, the funeral must focus on the living God and not on a dead body. It is best to have the casket closed. When the funeral is held in the church sanctuary, it is possible even to have the congregation participate in the reading of Scripture (if pew Bibles are available) or a responsive reading from the back of the hymnal. Some churches include a congregational hymn in the service. This decision should be left to the family, since church traditions differ.

A second purpose for the funeral is to *dignify man*. Man is made in the image of God, and the body of the believer is the temple of God, sealed by the Holy Spirit "unto the day of redemption" (Eph. 4:30; cf. 1:13-14). The body will one day be raised in glory, so there is no excuse for disposing of it in ignominy. Throughout the Bible, believing people tenderly cared for their dead and gave them honorable burial. Salvation involves the whole person, and that includes the body.

Of course, every Christian knows that the body is merely the "tent" in which the deceased lived; but that body was important to the loved ones while the person was alive. To minimize that close relationship with a body is to minimize life itself. Husband and wife are "one flesh," and the death of a marriage partner is a devastating experience both physically and emotionally. Trite phrases like "Rejoice, she's in heaven now!" or "He wouldn't want to come back if he could" only compound the grief and make God the "winner" and God's people on earth the losers.

The message of the funeral ought to remind the listeners that life is the gift of God and that death is real. There must be a finality to it that says to the mourners, "We must build a new relationship, because the old relationship is ended." True healing cannot begin until the mourners accept that fact and move forward.

It is possible to dignify man and glorify God at the same time, for God made man in His image and, in the life of the believer, is restoring that image. While the old-fashioned eulogy is, for the most part, no longer a part of our funeral services, there is certainly nothing wrong with giving honor where honor is due. It glorifies God when the life of a man or woman has been invested in things eternal, in service to others, and in the pursuit of godliness.

The third purpose of the funeral is to *testify to our faith*. It is a time of witness as well as a time of worship. This does not mean that the entire service is a high-powered evangelistic meeting during which we take advantage of the stirred emotions of people and "compel them to come in." If the music, Scripture readings, prayers, and message are carefully planned and presented in the power of the Spirit, there will be a powerful witness given as well as comfort shared with the mourners.

The funeral service ought to present the Christian view of both life and death. Christ should be magnified and the message of the gospel made crystal clear. The power of the blessed hope ought to grip every heart. The ideal funeral service ought to send people away saying, "Surely the Lord is in this place; and I knew it not!" (Gen. 28:16).

Finally, the funeral service should *fortify those who mourn*. The ministry is for the living, not for the dead. Bereaved persons feel very lonely, and the funeral service permits friends and loved ones to gather around them and encourage them. The very presence of caring people is a ministry in itself. It provides the right kind of setting for worship and the ministry of the Word. It also provides the right atmosphere for honest mourning.

The presence of loving friends and relatives encourages the grieving family to express itself honestly. There is no need to put on a front when people are sharing grief and "weeping with them that weep." Christians sorrow, but not as those who have no hope (1 Thess. 4:13-18); and they are not afraid to express their sorrow when supported in their pain by people who understand and love. The Fact that God knows and understands how we feel is at the foundation of all grief therapy and the healing of broken hearts. God's love is expressed most tangibly by God's people, and the funeral service gives opportunity for the expression of this love.

In recent years, however, it has been evident that even Christians do not attend funerals. Many friends and church members find it more convenient to attend the visitation the evening before the funeral. That is understandable. Not everybody can afford to miss work in order to attend a funeral service, and those who are not employed often have other responsibilities to fulfill.

But the local church family needs to understand the importance of *supportive fellowship* at the funeral. Some churches provide baby-sitting service so that young mothers may attend funerals. One of the best testimonies to unsaved relatives is the presence of God's people, sharing the grief of one whom they love. Although the pastor cannot organize a mourners' band or force people to attend the funeral, he can remind his church family of the importance of their presence at the service.

Most dedicated believers would want their pastor to conduct services that achieve these goals, but there are other people who would try to avoid such high and holy purposes. There are five kinds of funeral services that the minister of the Word must seek to avoid.

1. *The secular funeral.* This is merely a humanistic and philosophical service that contains no message of hope for the deceased of the bereaved. It is the feeling of some pastoral psychology students that the secular funeral (with the funeral director in charge) is the wave of the future. After all, why should a person who avoided church when he or she was alive be ushered out of this life by means of a religious service? It seems that honesty and integrity would demand that the service be suited to the life and beliefs of the deceased.

But it is possible to have a secular funeral even in the name of the Lord, simply by avoiding saying anything that might offend the listeners. Although a funeral service is not the place to defend the faith, it certainly is an opportunity for declaring the faith. The minister who tries to be all things to all mourners, who preaches every deceased person into heaven, and who assures the mourners that a loving God would never condemn anybody, is promoting paganism and secularism under the guise of Christianity.

2. *The superstitious funeral.* Fortunately, this kind of service is disappearing; but occasionally a family will request things to be done that simply are not Christian, but superstitious. The casket must face a certain direction. Members of the family must deposit a personal item in the casket before it is closed. A certain amount of wailing is demanded of each mourner. Although it is impossible for a pastor to change people's minds or tell them what to do, he must work with the funeral director to try to keep things under control. What cannot be changed must be endured, and then he must trust God to use his ministry to overcome whatever un-Christian elements are present in the funeral.

3. *The superficial funeral.* We attended the funeral service

for a retired man who was fairly well known; and yet not once during the service did the minister mention the name of the deceased! The entire service was superficial and anonymous. Granted, the minister did not know the deceased personally; but he at least could have mentioned his name, and family members would gladly have given him information about their loved one.

We are ministering to real people who have experienced a real loss. The deceased is a real person. Even if the deceased is a stranger to us personally, we must make every effort to learn some significant things about him or her, and to make the service as personal as possible.

The service must also deal with *death* realistically. To beat around the bush and use euphemisms for death is to make the ministry superficial. To be sure, we do not want to be brutal; and the Bible does speak of death as "sleep" and of departure as being "with Christ" (at least for the believer). But none of these images of death was given to minimize either the reality of death or the sorrow that comes to the hearts of the survivors.

Finally, the service must challenge the people to return to life with its duties and to face courageously the days ahead. A message of hope must deal honestly with the realities of loneliness, anger, frustration, and doubt. As we have noted, true comfort is a fortifying experience, not an experience of escape.

4. *The sentimental funeral.* Someone has defined *sentiment* as "feeling without responsibility." True sentiment can be a beautiful thing, but mere *sentimentality* is an emotional cop-out that eventually leaves the bereaved feeling worse than before. The sentimental person displays his or her emotions, not to express true feelings, but to impress those who are watching. These emotions are not only cheap, but they are counterfeit. Too often they are covering up the real feelings of the person, and that can create serious problems.

There was a time when sentimental preaching was expected at funerals. The minister imagined the deceased in heaven, greeting relatives and friends, and even sending messages back to his grieving family. The funeral message contained more heat than light, but it helped the bereaved to give vent to their emotions, real or spurious. Fortunately, that kind of preaching is not in vogue today; and we hope it never will be.

5. *The sensational funeral.* This is sentimentality taken to extremes. The funeral is not a worship service; rather, it is a production to satisfy the curious and the calloused, at the expense of the bereaved. If the deceased was a suicide or a murder victim, or if the story of the death was in the newspapers, then it is likely that a group of sensation-seeking people will show up for the service. The last thing we need at a funeral is a company of curiosity-seekers who want to be entertained.

The best thing to do is to avoid them. It may be that some word from the Lord will even penetrate a hard heart and do some good. The minister's task is to comfort the mourning, not to tickle the ears of the careless. Fortunately, the demands of human life have made it more difficult for the sensation seekers to attend most funerals, and this problem is rapidly diminishing.

Somebody must be in charge of the funeral service, and it had better be the minister. He may have to give in to certain harmless requests, but he alone must set the tone and determine the contents of the service. This can be done in a way that both pleases the family and honors the Lord. If the minister is a godly person, with sincere love for his people, there should be little difficulty.

We will never conduct the perfect funeral, nor will we ever reach the high ideals that we set for ourselves. The service that we think has been a failure may turn out to accomplish far more than we ever hoped. We must do our best and leave the results with the Lord. We must see to it that each service is unique and personal, that we are not merely dipping into the barrel and using the same messages, prayers, music, and order of service time after time. The minister who walks with God and lives with his people will always know what to do, and will do it to glorify God.

7

The Funeral Message

Christian people expect to hear something from God's Word when they are going through the valley. The funeral message, if it points to Christ and illumines the Word, can do much to bring encouragement and comfort to grieving people. God's Word is the only book that gives authoritative information about life and death, and we had better heed what it says.

The funeral message is not like any other message that the minister proclaims. It must be biblical, and it must be organized; but it must not "sound like a sermon," either in organization or presentation. The message must present *one truth*, in a vivid manner, so that the listeners may understand it and appropriate it for themselves.

The presentation should be *quiet and conversational*, as though the minister were simply talking with the family in their living room. The funeral message is no place for oratory or technical theological terms, including Greek and Hebrew words. We recall one minister who felt it necessary to explain the meaning of *parakletos*, and another pastor who decided to give a theological lecture on the resurrection, based on 1 Corinthians 15. Neither message brought much comfort, except when it ended.

The message should be *positive*, sharing with the listeners what the Bible clearly teaches. The message should also be *personal*, prepared with the deceased and the mourners in mind. One pastor used "Christ the Carpenter" as his theme, when conducting the service for a man who had worked all his life in the carpentry trade. The message pointed out that Jesus came to build and that today He is building a home in heaven for those who have trusted Him.

If the minister focuses on one central biblical truth and illumines it in a practical way, he should have little trouble keeping his message under ten minutes in length. The text itself should be brief, and it should be a verse that states the truth in a clear and imaginative way. A text that demands too much explanation will never do the job. Few mourners are prepared for an exegetical discussion. They need medicine for their hearts, not theological prescriptions.

The message should *center on God and His grace* and not on man and his failures. The message must look ahead and be radiant with hope. At the same time, it must be realistic and let the listeners know that death is real, that grief hurts, and that life is not easy. The preacher must convey, by both his words and his attitude, that God understands how they feel and that He is with them.

The message is preached for the good of the living and not for the glory of the dead. It is a message, not a eulogy; and it must lift the hearts of the mourners to that which is heavenly and eternal. It is wise not to preach anybody into either heaven or hell: the Lord knows those that are His. Had Judas died before the triumphal entry into Jerusalem, no doubt Peter would have preached him into paradise. Although we have a reasonable certainty about most professed Christians, we must still exercise caution. And certainly we must be careful not to condemn those who seemingly made no profession. We never know what transpires between the soul and God during those final minutes of human life.

Perhaps the one word that best describes the ideal funeral message is *sensitivity*. The minister must be sensitive to the needs of the family and to the testimony (or lack of it) of the deceased. He must be sensitive to the truth of the Word and apply it in a sensitive way to those who listen. The funeral message must turn the listeners' ears into eyes so that they *see* the truth pictured in a vivid way. Experience plus complete dependence on the Spirit of God will equip the devoted pastor for this kind of ministry. If he loves his people, he will know how to minister to their hearts.

How does the pastor go about selecting the text for the message? If the deceased has been ailing for a long time, then the death would not likely be a surprise; and there is no reason the minister should not have some texts in mind. This is especially important when the deceased is a valued member of the church, perhaps an officer.

Each pastor should have a file of "luminous texts" that he has met with in his Bible reading and sermon preparation, texts that strike him as ideal for funeral messages. Andrew Blackwood called this the "sermonic seed bed," and it is a good description. From time to time, he will get insights into some of these texts, and he will add to his file. When he suddenly finds himself faced with a funeral, and perhaps only two days in which to prepare, he turns to this file, reviews the texts and the notes, and seeks a text that suits the situation.

It is important that the text convey spiritual truth and not simply be used as a Christian motto. If the context of the passage must be explained in detail before the text makes sense, then avoid that text. Many church people are biblically illiterate these days, and the outsiders who attend funerals would not have much opportunity to grasp the finer points of exegesis. The minister who sticks to clear, simple texts that deal with timeless truths will end up with the best message that meets the most needs.

For example, Psalm 116:15 is often used as a funeral text— "Precious in the sight of the Lord is the death of his saints." But usually the text is used totally apart from its context, and that gives people the impression that God *enjoys* seeing people die and come to heaven! When you read the entire psalm, you discover that the writer had been in great danger, but had cried out to God and been delivered. Why? Because the death of God's children is a precious thing to the Lord, something that *He* plans and executes. His children do not die by accident, but by appointment. All of this needs to be explained before verse 15 really makes sense. A careless use of the verse can easily give people the wrong idea of both God and death. After all, people are also precious to us, and we hate to lose them.

The minister should also avoid looking for biblical parallels to either the life or the death of the deceased. For one thing, it takes too long to present that much material; but even more, the parallels may break down or turn out to be false. The account of the death of David and Bathsheba's baby does contain some spiritual truths that are useful for the preacher, but the story could also arouse feelings of guilt. "God took our baby because we sinned!"

Certainly a faithful church officer can be compared with Barnabas, "the son of encouragement" (Acts 11:24); that text needs little explanation. We must also avoid idealizing the deceased by using texts that refer to the great men and women of the Bible. We should select texts that minister to the sorrowing, not glorify the deceased.

Imagination is a great tool for sermon preparation, but it must never be permitted to become *fancy*. The minister who twists a text just to make it fit the situation is sinning against God, himself, and the people who are looking to him for help and comfort. The pastor who used Hebrews 12:1-2 at the service for a railroad man ("he has made his last run") was only exposing his ignorance and inviting ridicule.

However, imagination can link golden texts with real-life situations and help to illumine the darkness in the valley. One pastor used Numbers 21:11 (KJV*) as the basis for a funeral message for a man who was a great outdoorsman and camper: "And they journeyed . . . and pitched . . . toward the sunrising." He pointed out that the human body is but a temporary tent (2 Cor. 5:1-4), and that life is a pilgrimage. The believer pitches his tent toward the sunrise, walking in the light; until finally he leaves his tent and enters heaven and a permanent home. "The path of the just is as the shining light, that shineth more and more unto the perfect day" (Prov. 4:18). The message was imaginative and biblical, but not fanciful. It was vivid enough for the people to see the truth and apply it.

By the way, as a general rule, it is best for the pastor to use the translation that is most familiar and meaningful to the people at the funeral. Nothing can match the beauty of the King James Version, although the *New King James Version*

* King James Version.

comes very close. We do not think that a funeral service is the place for the pastor to introduce controversial translations. The family may request a certain translation or version, and the pastor should cooperate, unless, of course, the version is heretical. Familiar passages such as Psalm 23, John 14, and 1 Thessalonians 4:13-18 are written lovingly on the hearts of many people, especially the older saints; and we gain little by using new translations that are unfamiliar.

There is always the temptation in a funeral message to emphasize the "vanity of life," but that temptation must be mastered. Life in Christ is *not* vain (1 Cor. 15:58), even though that life may be brief on earth. Remember, one purpose of the funeral service is to declare the *value of life*. If life is not precious, why weep over those who have died? Let the message be realistic: life is precious, death is painful, and only in Christ can we have true comfort.

Although it is true that "to depart and be with Christ is far better," the preacher must keep in mind that the truth applies to the deceased, not to the survivors. In fact, Paul even said so: "Nevertheless to abide in the flesh is more needful for you" (Phil. 1:23-24). The fact that the deceased is better off does not mean that the survivors feel better now that their loved one is dead! In our minds, we affirm the truth of the Word; but in our hearts, we hurt very deeply. Even if the deceased suffered greatly or was severely injured, we still feel the loss, though we know the person is better off in heaven.

There was a time when God's saints meditated on heaven and talked and sang much about it; but that is not the situation today. Unfortunately, about the only time Christians discuss heaven is when someone in the family or church is dangerously ill, or there has been a death in the family. As far as believers today are concerned (except for a very small minority), heaven is the place we go after we have had a good time here on earth!

But to the saints of Bible history, heaven was not just a destination; it was *a motivation* (see Hebrews 11:10-14, 16, 26, 35). The people of God built their whole lives on the vision of further glory. We must be careful not to make heaven look like the last cop-out. There is not sufficient time at a funeral service to develop a biblical doctrine of heaven, but the faithful minister will certainly give that necessary instruction to his people in the course of his regular ministry. In our modern scientific world, many people are asking serious questions about life after life and this place called "heaven," and they deserve biblical answers. Heaven will certainly be a place of worship (Rev. 4-5, 19:1-8), service (Rev. 7:15; 22:3), reigning (Rev. 5:10), fellowship (Heb. 12:23; Rev. 19:9), rest (Rev. 14:13), and glorifying God (Eph. 1:10-12). It is "my Father's house" (John 14:1-6), the place where God's family will gather forever (Ps. 23:6).

Perhaps something needs to be said about the preaching of the doctrine of hell and eternal punishment. That there is a hell awaiting unbelievers is a motivating force in evangelism (Luke 16:27-28). Our Lord preached about hell, even in the Sermon on the Mount (Matt. 5:22 and 5:29-30). As far as the record is concerned, our Lord had more to say about hell than He did about heaven. Although the apostle Paul never used the word *gehenna* in his writings, and used *hades* only once (1 Cor. 15:55), he did write about "everlasting destruction," anguish, tribulation, wrath to come, death, condemnation, and punishment. He believed in the reality of hell.

But how do we preach about hell at a funeral service? How do we warn the lost to "flee from the wrath to come"? It is not likely that we will major on that theme, or that we will want to use the kind of vivid language that our godly forefathers used. "In order that nothing may be wanting to the happiness of the blessed in heaven," wrote Thomas Aquinas, "a perfect view is granted them of the torture of the damned" (*Treatise on The Last Things*, Question XCIV, Article 1).

Even Charles Spurgeon waxed eloquent on the subject: "Thy body will lie, asbestos-like, forever unconsumed, all thy veins roads for the feet of Pain to travel on, every nerve a string on which the Devil shall forever play his diabolical tune of hell's unutterable lament" (quoted in *Fundamentals of the Faith*, edited by Carl F. H. Henry, p. 239*). And Jonathan Edwards said, "The view of the misery of the damned will double the ardour of the love and gratitude of the saints in heaven" (*Miscellanies*, p. 279).

Whatever truth may be found in the statements of those great men, this much is sure: we are not likely today to get

* Grand Rapids: Zondervan, 1969.

much of a positive response if we imitate their approach. That kind of lurid oratory is suspect in today's propaganda-saturated world, and we wonder if the funeral service is the place for it anyway. This is not to suggest that we preach a false peace or that we fail to warn the sinner. Rather, it is to suggest that we be "wise as serpents and harmless as doves."

It is true that things like the Holocaust and the constant threat of nuclear attack have made people today more conscious of judgment, but we doubt that most unsaved people relate either of these grim realities to eternal hell. They may think about the tragic destruction of life, but not about eternal condemnation after death. In a world that caricatures Satan and hell, many people do not take such things seriously.

Theological liberalism has managed to do away with eternal punishment and give to modern sinners several comfortable substitutes. Universalism is one of them, that all men will eventually be saved. Another is annihilationism, that the lost are eventually destroyed so that they do not suffer endlessly. A second chance after death is another false hope of the lost. As one liberal writer put it, "God has no permanent problem children."

Modern man sees criminals go free when they ought to be condemned, and he has a hard time believing in divine judgment. The overemphasis on the love of God has almost obliterated the doctrine of the holiness of God. Modern man thinks of punishment in terms of reformation, not retribution. It is for the good of the criminal, not for the upholding of the law. God certainly is not less loving than a federal judge!

A funeral service is no place to argue about either heaven or hell or to give a theological lecture on either; but it is a place to bear witness of Bible truth and to speak that truth in love. We may not choose to use the word hell, but we certainly ought to declare the fact that death is the end of all opportunity for salvation, and that judgment awaits the person who has rejected Christ. The good news of salvation must include the bad news of condemnation; otherwise there is no good news to tell.

But the loving pastor will not exploit his listeners at a time when their emotions are already in turmoil. He will seek *positive* ways to bear witness to the truth, and he will allow the

Scriptures to speak for themselves. There is a loving way to present even the most difficult doctrines, and the mature minister will meditate, pray, and ask God to show him the best way. R. W. Dale, who did not believe in eternal punishment for the wicked, once said that D. L. Moody was the only preacher he ever heard who had the right to preach about hell, because Moody always spoke of hell with tears. Alas, some well-meaning ministers preach about hell as though they were glad people are going there.

The Scriptures mentioned in chapter 4 are suitable for funeral messages. In fact, almost any Scripture that touches a human need and reveals a divine truth can be used to comfort the bereaved.

Here are a few more texts that you may add to your "sermonic seed-plot" and cultivate:

> Exodus 16:7—seeing God's glory in the morning
> 1 Samuel 1:27-28—the child given to the Lord
> 1 Samuel 20:3—only a step to death (and to life!)
> 2 Samuel 12:23—the death of an infant
> Psalm 77:9—when a family has had tragedy after tragedy
> Proverbs 4:18—the lightened pathway of the just
> Proverbs 10:7—the memory of the just
> Proverbs 16:31—for an aged saint (see also Isaiah 46:4)
> Proverbs 31:30-31—a godly mother
> Ecclesiastes 3:11—everything is beautiful *in its time*
> Isaiah 40:11—God's special care for the lambs (a child)
> Isaiah 61:1-2—(Luke 4:16-19) healing the broken-hearted
> Jeremiah 15:9—"her sun is gone down while it was yet day" (text for the death of a young lady)
> Matthew 18:10—heaven's care for the child
> Mark 10:13-16—Jesus welcomes the little children
> John 11:28—the call of the Master
> John 11:32—"Lord, if—"
> John 13:7—"thou shalt know hereafter"
> Romans 8:38-39—even death cannot keep us from God's love

1 Corinthians 13:12—one day we shall understand
Hebrews 9:17—death is an appointment, not an accident

Later in this book we shall give some suggested outlines
for funeral messages, some of which will be based on a selection
from this list of texts.

The message is but one part of the funeral service. There
are other elements to be considered.

THE MUSIC

If the service is in the church sanctuary or chapel, the
church musicians will no doubt participate. The family of the
deceased may choose to ask someone in the church family to
play and/or sing. That kind of loving participation can be meaningful and an encouragement to the sorrowing. We would much
rather listen to an average amateur musician minister in love
than to an imported professional present a recital.

The choice of songs should be made by the family; the
minister should make suggestions only if he feels they have
made some unwise choices. How the matter is handled depends
a great deal on the kind of relationship the pastor has with the
family. A beloved shepherd who cares for his people will have
little difficulty encouraging them to follow his leading.

The order of service will probably be left up to the minister,
and he should be careful not to use a carbon-copy liturgy that
is predictable. Of course, much depends on the number of songs
being used and whether or not the family wishes an obituary
read. Here are some suggested orders of service.

#1—No Musical Selections
Prelude
Call to worship
Invocation (mention name of the deceased)
Scripture
Message
Closing pastoral prayer
Benediction
Postlude

#2—One Musical Selection

Prelude	
Call to worship	
Invocation	*Alternative*
Scripture	Musical selection
Musical selection	Scripture
Message	Pastoral prayer
Pastoral prayer	Message
Benediction	Benediction

Another possibility is to have the second musical selection after the message and then close with the benediction.

If there is to be an obituary (or eulogy), it can be given just after the invocation. It is best to put the obituary early in the service so that the people may easily identify with the deceased, and also so that the minister may lead them from there into an ascending vision of God as they worship together. After the invocation, the minister may simply say: "We have met today to honor the life and memory of ——" and then procede with the obituary. The transition from obituary to Scripture may be: "This is the earthly record. Now shall we hear the heavenly message that our hearts need today."

The pastor should be flexible, however. We have occasionally worked the obituary into the funeral message itself, but this is not easy to do—nor should it be done too often. Whatever order of service is used, it should as much as possible blend the elements of worship in such a way that there is no jarring note or difficult transition. Liturgy is not an end in itself but a means to an end; and in this case, that purpose is to glorify God as we minister comfort to hurting people.

THE SCRIPTURES

We have already suggested various Scriptures that may be used, and the family may have further suggestions. Whatever Scriptures are read, they should focus on life and God's grace and glory, and not on death and the frailty of man. In particular, the verse or verses used for the call to worship must center the congregation's heart and mind on God and His gift of abundant life in Christ. Many of the texts already mentioned may be used. We have often used 1 John 3:1-2 because of its emphasis on God's love, salvation, and future glory. First Peter 1:3-4 is another arresting text.

We do not believe that the regular Scripture reading should be long. Although there is much to be learned from John 11 and 1 Corinthians 15, we do not suggest that you read these chapters in their entirety, or even long paragraphs from them. John 11:21-27 is a good selection, and 1 Corinthians 15:51-58 gives a good summary of the resurrection hope. (However, you may want to use it at the grave, along with verses 42-44.)

The spiritually alert pastor will know just what texts will help his people the most, and he will put them together into a beautiful compilation that will blend together in a balanced way. Although he may find many suggestions in a minister's service manual, he will prefer to assemble his own texts and read them, rather than depend on what others have used.

Rather than fill his Bible with numerous markers, and have to turn pages, the minister should make use of the office copying machine and assemble his Scriptures in compact form. Better still, he should commit them to memory or be so familiar with them that he will not be chained to a manuscript or Bible.

No matter how familiar the texts may be, the minister should take time to saturate his soul with God's Word so that his sharing of the Word will be meaningful and not routine. Few things are as deadening to a worship service as the humdrum reading of Scripture in a mechanical fashion. This is the living Word of God! It must be read with heart and meaningful interpretation. This is God's message to broken hearts! It must not be made dull and ordinary.

PRAYER

The invocation should be brief, but personal. It is usually good to mention the name of the deceased, but this can vary from service to service. "As we meet to remember —, our Father, be to us the God of all grace and the God of all comfort, through Jesus Christ our Lord, Amen."

Another possibility is to mention the deceased after the call to worship. "We have met today to worship our living Lord, and to pay our respects to —. Let us pray." Then follows the invocation.

Like the Scripture reading, the pastoral prayer must not

become routine. The minister should prepare it (not necessarily write it out word for word) and have some key phrases before him to guide him as he prays. He must truly *pray* and not "preach over the Lord's shoulder." Although there are some beautiful prayers available in various worship manuals, including the *Book of Common Prayer*, the creative pastor will benefit from them but not imitate them. He will want to pray "in the Spirit," trusting God to guide him as he prepares; and he will try to make the prayer meet the needs of those to whom he is ministering.

The pastoral prayer need not be long, but it should be full. It must include the important aspects of prayer: adoration, confession, thanksgiving, and intercession. The minister must gather the flock together as he prays and bring them in love and faith to the Great Shepherd of the sheep.

Should he mention names in his prayer? Again, it depends on the strength of his relationship to the family. If he plans to mention the names of the bereaved personally—at least, the immediate family—then he should have those names before him, lest he forget someone. If the family is a large one, he had better not try to mention all the names; or if some distant relative is likely to be offended by being omitted. The members of a smaller and more intimate family certainly may be prayed for one by one.

THE OBITUARY

The obituary is omitted in many services today. But if the family requests it, or if local custom requires it, then it must be included. However, it must not be permitted to get too long; and the minister and funeral director must be certain that the facts are correct. The best way to be sure is to check with a knowledgeable family member well in advance. Even the best kept records can contain mistakes.

The minister will want to go over the obituary and make sure that he is pronouncing all names correctly. Again, a cooperating family member or close friend of the family can be very helpful.

Although the minister should always ask if the family wishes an obituary read, he should not press for it. If there is no obituary, the minister will certainly want to include facts about the deceased in his funeral message. The funeral service must not be anonymous.

OTHER ELEMENTS

Sometimes the family (or a family member) will want to include a favorite poem. If the poem is a good one, and not merely a piece of sentimental doggerel, then the minister must decide where to use it. Sometimes a poem with a spiritual message can be used in the funeral sermon or as a transition from one part of the service to another.

But sometimes the family may request a poem that the pastor would rather not use. What shall he do? We recall one family that asked the minister to read a "philosophical poem" that really carried no spiritual message. He did the wise thing: he read the poem very early in the service, and followed it with the reading of the Scriptures. The contrast was devastating— and the Scriptures won!

If the deceased belonged to an organization that conducts funeral rites, it is best to let them have their service totally apart from the Christian funeral. Most organization chaplains are happy to have their service the evening before, at the close of the wake; and some will do it just before the minister takes over. Military chaplains are only too happy to cooperate with the pastor in charge if he will give them the opportunity.

Some ministers have made it clear to their people that they will not participate in fraternal rites that have religious overtones, lest they compromise the witness of the gospel. If the deceased was not a part of the church family, the minister may have no option but to make the best of his opportunity and be as wise as a serpent but as harmless as a dove.

Perhaps the family will ask another clergyman or even a lay person to participate in the service. The deceased's pastor should be in charge, however, and should conduct the service. The guest may read Scripture, or even give the message; but it should be clear that the local pastor is in charge. It is his responsibility to see that the overall atmosphere of the service is worshipful and glorifies God. He should let the guest know the order of the service and the time limits involved.

ALTERNATE SERVICES

So far, we have been discussing the traditional funeral. There are other kinds of services.

The *private funeral* involves limited attendance as determined by the family. When the family of a deceased public figure prefers to sorrow alone and avoid the glare of publicity, they plan a private service. Or, if the death of the person was somewhat sensational—murder, suicide, killed by the police— the family often wisely chooses to mourn privately. The minister, of course, must honor their requests.

We will consider special situations in the next section of this book, so we will not go into detail here. Suffice it to say that the minister must always do his best in seeking to heal the brokenhearted, no matter how the loved one may have died. We are called to be witnesses, not judges or prosecuting attorneys. The minister must also be careful to keep confidence. There will always be people looking for news or gossip after the service ends.

The *memorial service* is basically a funeral without the presence of the body of the deceased. The body may have been donated to science, or cremated and the ashes scattered, or perhaps never found. (That is sometimes the case with drownings.) Many psychologists believe that the presence of the body is important to the grief work of the mourners. They need to realize that the loved one is indeed dead and that the former relationship is ended. We must admit that there is a finality to the situation when the body is present and then interred at the cemetery, and this finality can assist the mourners as they deal with their feelings.

Often the family has a picture (or pictures) of the deceased at the memorial service, and that assists them in remembering him or her. Pictures are also used at traditional services when the casket remains closed.

A memorial service does have definite advantages. It can be planned for a time convenient for the most people, and there is no need to worry about either mortuary or cemetery schedules. The service may be held in the church or even in a home. The family and the minister have ample opportunity to make plans and prepare a service to honor the deceased in a proper manner. Finally, the absence of the body can help to give a more worshipful atmosphere to the service.

At a memorial service, the reading of the obituary (or eulogy) probably takes on greater significance. The body of the deceased is not present, and several days may have elapsed since the person died.

Sometimes the family will have a private burial service at the cemetery, and then gather days or weeks later for a memorial service. If there is a private cremation and disposal of the ashes, they may want their pastor present. Local laws dictate what may or may not be done to a corpse, including the disposing of the ashes.

Many memorial services involve addresses by several people: family members, business associates, church friends. These addresses can become highly eulogistic, and it is the minister's job to see to it that the service ultimately points to Christ. Even if the deceased was a believer, he or she probably had social or business associates who are not believers, people who might not fully understand that a memorial service is a time of worship. As the pastor prepares, he will want to make that clear in a nonthreatening way.

In some parts of the United States, *cremation* is becoming more acceptable to Christian people. Although there are probably more biblical arguments against the practice than for it, the pastor will accomplish little by debating with the family. If they ask his counsel, he can share his convictions in love; but he must not refuse to have anything to do with the service because he disagrees. Would he refuse to conduct a memorial service if the body were given to a medical school? Probably not. If he does have strong convictions about the matter (and not just prejudices), he should instruct his people *before* the crisis appears.

In most cases, there is a regular funeral service, and then the body is cremated. It takes about two hours for the body and casket to be reduced to ashes. These ashes are placed in a container, and they may be disposed of in one of three ways: (1) burial of the container in the family cemetery plot; (2) placing the urn in a niche in a columbarium, usually connected with the crematorium; or (3) scattering the ashes in a place meaningful to the memory of the deceased.

Unless the family requests it, the minister need not remain after he has concluded the service. In fact, the family may not even stay. However, they may want the pastor to assist them when they do dispose of the ashes. If not, he is free to include the committal in his closing words at the service.

Most Protestant denominations do not forbid cremation, although some discourage it. It is definitely not acceptable to the Greek Orthodox church and orthodox Jews. The Second Vatican Council has authorized priests to participate in cremation services when asked to do so, but the Roman Catholic church still prefers burial.

8

At the Grave

The purpose of the committal service at the grave is to write, "It is finished!" over all that has been done. There is a finality to death that the human heart must accept, no matter how difficult that acceptance may be.

When he arrives at the cemetery (usually with the funeral director), the minister joins the pallbearers and leads them and the family to the open grave. He waits until all the family and friends have gathered before he begins the service. This consists of the reading of the Scriptures, the actual committal, and then a closing prayer and benediction. The service need not be long. In fact, there are times when weather conditions force us to complete the service as quickly as possible.

We have always preferred to emphasize *the blessed hope* rather than the fact that man returns to dust. "The word *cemetery* means 'a sleeping place,' " the pastor might say. "It is the place where the body sleeps, awaiting the resurrection at the coming of Jesus Christ for His people. Sometimes the cemetery is called 'God's acre,' because here we plant the bodies into the ground just as you plant a seed." Here the reading of 1 Corinthians 15:42-44 would be appropriate.

"We sorrow today, but not as those who have no hope; for there will be a resurrection of the dead and a reunion of God's people." Here the minister may read either 1 Corinthians 15:51-

58 or 1 Thessalonians 4:13-18. It is not necessary to explain and expound; he should let the Word speak for itself.

After the reading of the Scriptures, he commits the body to the earth.

"Inasmuch as God in His sovereign will has called the soul of —— (if a believer, "called to Himself the soul of ——"), we now commit his/her body to the earth from which it came, earth to earth, ashes to ashes, dust to dust." He may want to sprinkle earth, or flower petals, on the casket as he says this. In fact, in some places it is the custom for family members to place flowers or petals on the casket when the minister says this. "And we commit his/her soul into the hands of our loving heavenly Father and our blessed Savior who said, 'I go to prepare a place for you.'"

He may then read Revelation 21:1-5 and close with prayer and a fitting benediction, perhaps Hebrews 13:20-21.

Of course, the pastor will suit his words to the situation. The best way to honor the dead is to care for the living. If the weather is bad, the pastor may certainly abbreviate the service without dishonoring the dead.

He should remain with the family at the grave and accompany them back to their cars. If his schedule permits, he may join them in any family fellowship that may have been planned, either in one of the homes or at the church.

As with most religious services, local customs differ; and the new pastor will want to find out in advance just what is expected at the graveside. In some places, the group will sing a familiar hymn; in other places, the service is closed with the people saying the Lord's Prayer. The important thing is that the service honor the Lord and show respect for the deceased, and that it minister to the family. It is not a time for wasting words.

An innovation has appeared in some cemeteries that can either help or hinder the committal service: the cemetery chapel. Instead of going to the graveside, the pallbearers take the casket into the chapel; and the committal service is held there. This is a great help in bad weather, but it can be a problem as far as the committal is concerned. The minister is not really committing the body to the "earth from which it came," and everybody knows it! And many people are wondering, "How will this body get to the grave and be buried?"

Personally, we prefer to have loved ones and friends carry the body to the grave, rather than have cemetery workers move it from the chapel on a cart or tractor. There is something *final* about being at the open grave, and this sense of finality is important to healthy mourning.

If the family prefers the cemetery chapel, then the pastor will certainly cooperate. But unless there is inclement weather, perhaps it is best to encourage the family (in advance) to have the body taken to the open grave. We recall more than one instance when the cemetery workers acted in haste, and the grieving family stood and beheld their loved one carted to the grave in a rather undignified fashion. Mourners have enough problems without manufacturing new ones for them.

It is always proper for the minister to thank the pallbearers and the funeral director privately for their help in the service.

Following the benediction, there may be an announcement about the further fellowship ("lunch at the church"). Such fellowship is a part of the healing process. If directions are necessary, ask the funeral director to provide a simple map. Copies of a map can even be made available at the service without detracting from the solemnity of the occasion.

9

Following the Funeral

Studies indicate that bereaved people need companionship and encouragement for weeks following the funeral or memorial service. Friends are prone to be helpful immediately after a death occurs and for a few days following the service; but then a new sorrow comes to the church family, and grieving people are too often neglected and forgotten. They often hit low ebb at about six weeks.

The minister must keep in touch. If convenient to the family, he should call in the home as soon as possible after the funeral; and he should make regular visits until he is sure that the grief work is going well and each person is learning to live with the loss in a mature and creative way.

The minister must not be the only one who is supporting the mourners, however; the church family must be taught to care. The first Sunday the grieving family is back in church, the pastor should take note of it, say something to the congregation, and include the sorrowing in his pastoral prayer. Although it may not be necessary to keep providing food and other things for six weeks after the funeral, there must be a continued support ministry that helps the grieving people to make the transition back into everyday life.

The minister must be alert for signs of trouble. The husband who "took it so well" at the funeral may start to have

physical problems. Parents who buried a child may begin to
have marital problems. The pastor needs to share the facts of
death and mourning with these people and let them know that
what they are experiencing is normal and can be handled successfully. They do not need lectures or books to read, but they
do need loving counsel from a trusted shepherd.

There is such a thing as extended grief, whe   the mourner
seems incapable of coming to grips with the situation and making a normal transition back into mature normal living. The
person is almost helpless and becomes more and more de-
pendent on others. In such cases, the pastor will want to encourage the mourner to seek professional help; and he himself
will try to be as supportive as possible.

What should the minister watch for as he visits the mourners in the days following the funeral? For one thing, their
willingness to talk about the deceased without "falling apart."
It is a good sign when memories can bring smiles as well as
tears. It is a very good sign when the person recognizes his or
her own responses to the grief situation. "Pastor, I'm just acting
like an old fool!" said one elderly mourner with a smile, and
that statement (and smile) signaled that she had turned the
corner.

Many sorrowing people have to face and overcome *regrets*.
We all know that we cannot change the past, but we can change
our attitudes toward the past, and thereby alter the present
and the future. Some people are so overcome with regret ("If
we had only called the doctor sooner!") that they live under a
cloud of self-condemnation; and sometimes they want to do
penance to atone for their failures. It may take several visits
and conversations to help them realize that (1) God knew all
about it, even before it happened; (2) God's love is not condi-
tioned on our perfection; (3) Romans 8:28 is still in the Bible;
(4) we can confess our sins and make a new beginning.

Post-funeral ministry is not easy, but it is necessary. One
big help is the fact that most mourners feel the need for pastoral
encouragement. However, the pastor must be careful not to
become a crutch that keeps the mourner from growing and
learning to accept life and live it to the glory of God.

Many people who lose loved ones get attached to the calendar and begin to notice anniversary dates. "Just three months

ago today Mother died." Wise is the pastor who keeps records, not only of the date of decease, but also birthdays ("Dad would have been fifty today") and anniversaries ("We would have been married fifty years today"). Obviously, this must not become a "sacred ritual," lest we get so attached to the past we fail to enjoy the present or plan for the future. But many people are very sentimental about such things, and they appreciate it when their pastor remembers.

It is also good for the church family to remember. Often the family will have flowers in the sanctuary on the anniversary of a loved one's death, and that gives the church family opportunity to affirm their love and also to remember the deceased brother or sister with gratitude to God for their life and ministry. The pastor will certainly want to make mention of the occasion from the pulpit.

Part 3

Special Situations

Men cannot live without meaning.
> (Albert Camus)

There is no waste of time in life like that of making
explanations.
> (Benjamin Disraeli)

The sky is not less blue because the blind man does
not see it.
> (Danish Proverb)

The quest for certainty blocks the search
for meaning.
> (Erich Fromm)

What I do you do not realize now, but you
shall understand hereafter.
> (Jesus to Peter—John 13:7, NASB)

10

The Pastor's Approach

Death is always an interruption, and some deaths are an invasion. The sudden death of a baby, the accidental death of a child, the murder of a young mother, all of these bring with them special problems and needs that can never be dealt with routinely. Ministers sometimes talk about "problem funerals" (a phrase we personally do not like, but we know what they mean), and it is these special situations that we want to address in this section.

Basically, the minister may take one of three approaches to a special funeral. First, he may ignore the special problems and hope that something he says meets the need. But if he does, he is likely to give the impression that he really cannot minister to the family's needs. "Everybody sitting in the funeral parlor knew that my husband committed suicide, but the preacher said nothing about it. How come?"

Or, the minister may try to explain the situation; but that is also a lost cause. To begin with, only God knows how and why these things happen, and it is dangerous for the preacher to "play God." But even if he can give a rational explanation for the murder of a husband or the crib death of a baby, explanations do not heal a broken heart. It is our strong conviction that people live on promises, not on explanations.

Instead of avoiding the problems or trying to explain them,

the minister should *interpret the situation* in the light of God's Word. As an interpreter, he assures the family that he understands their feelings, especially their perplexity. But he also assures them that God will meet their needs even if He does not immediately answer all of their questions. They do not need better reasons; they need better relationships with the Lord and with their situation.

Admitting that we do not know *why* is not a confession that we do not know *anything*. The wise man knows what he does *not* know and does not try to fool anybody into thinking that he knows more. God has not explained everything to us, but He has revealed enough to us so that we can live by faith, make sensible decisions, and enjoy what He has planned for us. "The secret things belong to the Lord our God, but the things revealed belong to us and to our sons forever, that we may observe all the words of this law" (Deut. 29:29, NASB).

Our approach, then, is that of *interpretation*, not explanation. The funeral message must be an emotional and spiritual catalyst that helps the mourner see himself or herself, see the Lord, and see the resources available for facing life courageously. The interpreter does not avoid the problems present, but he puts them into the much larger setting of the worship of God. He hears the burning questions in the mourners' hearts, and he accepts them; but he does not try to give pat answers or theological explanations. He ministers to the heart, knowing that there will be time enough in the days to come to answer the questions in the mind.

In facing the situation honestly, the pastor must not go to the extreme of being brutally realistic. It is not necessary to use the words *suicide* or *murder* every other sentence just to get the point across. In fact, he can face the issue and not even use the words. "All of us are asking, 'Why should a thing like this happen?'" is a statement that lets people know the preacher is being honest. Words like suicide and murder can cut into the already broken hearts of loved ones and only add to their agony.

In this section, we can give only a summary of what the pastor may do and say. We suggest that the concerned reader consult the books in the bibliography for more detailed treatments of these special matters.

11

The Death of a Child

Sudden Infant Death Syndrome (SIDS) is the number one cause of death among children from one week to five years of age; and the majority of those deaths (for some reason) occur during the six coldest months of the year. SIDS will strike three out of every thousand infants in the United States, and the mystery that surrounds these deaths can create serious problems in homes. In more than one instance, parents have blamed themselves, the baby-sitter, and even the other children in the family, when even the doctor does not know who or what is to blame.

The death of an infant or child usually hits the mother the hardest. She has lived with the child for nine months with the kind of expectancy that grows as the time of birth draws near. When a newborn baby dies, the mother's normal response might well be, "Was it worth it all? Why would God give me nine months of life and then shatter my hopes? It all seems so futile!"

Sometimes the mother is unable to attend the funeral service, and that further complicates the problem. Many hospitals wisely move the mother to a new location so that the presence of the other mothers and new babies will not upset her; but she still knows they are there.

That is not to say that the father is untouched, but he

usually has so many things to do that his deepest feelings may
not show up until after the crisis when the mother is safely
home. His first concern will be his wife, as well as the other
children, if there are any.

The death of a child can produce problems in the marriage.
Studies indicate that 90 percent of the bereaved couples have
marital difficulties within a few months after the child's death.
It is possible in some cases that the bereavement *revealed* the
problems rather than caused them; but in any case, the difficulties must be dealt with.

The father is usually busy on the job, while the grieving
mother is left at home with reminders and memories. Even in
her most intimate relations with her husband, she may be reminded that the fruit of her womb was taken from her. If there
are siblings, the couple faces another set of challenges. It requires a great deal of love, patience, and prayer for a grieving
couple to get through the valley and emerge again into the
sunshine.

What we have written in part 1 about the grieving process
applies here. The couple must be given time to work through
their feelings about the child and its death. There are two approaches to the situation that they want to avoid: (1) keeping
everything as it was—the "Little Boy Blue" syndrome—and (2)
trying to erase every reminder and memory. The answer is
neither in preserving the past nor eradicating it. The answer
is in accepting the past and learning from it, letting it become
a rudder to guide them but not an anchor to hold them back.
Memories become richer and more meaningful as the years
pass, and it is a shame to lose them or waste them.

What about the other children in the home? How do they
face and handle grief? Most psychologists believe that children
from one to five *deny* the reality of death. In our media-satu-
rated world, it is impossible for them not to be confronted with
death; but the whole experience is unreal to them. Yes, people
are shot and killed in the comics and on TV, but nobody takes
it seriously.

From ages five to nine, children accept the reality of death,
but they really do not understand what takes place, and they
are not sure it will happen to them. At about age nine or ten,
the child realizes that, even for him, death is inevitable.

Certainly a child's grief at the loss of a loved one is just as real as the grief experienced by an adult. We may smile at their tears and say, "They don't understand"; but does *anybody* understand? We must accept their grief and let them know that we accept it. Their vessels may be small, but they can still be filled with sorrow.

Some studies reveal that the child's first response to the death of a loved one is *protest*—this cannot and shall not happen! This is the *anger* stage, and it is sometimes mixed with fantasy. "This is just a dream, a joke. My mommy will come back!" This attitude can easily turn into bitter hostility: "Why did Daddy do this! If he loved us, he would have stayed with us and not died!"

The second stage is *pain*. The child's world falls apart as he or she realizes that the loved one *is* gone and will not come back. If the grief work is normal, the child will move into the third stage, *promise*. He or she begins to get things organized, hope moves into the heart, and the child decides that life will have to go on. That is not to say that all the feelings have been resolved and all the questions answered; but it does mean that life is returning to normal.

Again, the greatest need is for acceptance and love, the kind of assurance that lets the child know that somebody cares. We recall having to explain to a ten-year-old girl that her father had committed suicide. We discovered later that what we said probably was not heard but the fact that we cared, we wept, and we accepted her response did more good than anything else.

If children do not seem to be expressing grief openly, it may be that they are doing so privately or with their peers. Or, they may be adopting a stoical attitude in hopes it will encourage their grieving parents. "I don't want to make Mommy and Daddy hurt anymore." Parents need to explain to their children that tears are a normal part of the grieving process, and that by expressing our feelings, we help the healing process. Children must not be *forced* to grieve, but they must be *free* to grieve; and the family that weeps together will more quickly heal together.

How do we explain death to a child? By being open and honest and not giving the child more than he or she can digest

intellectually or emotionally. It is important that we not give
the impression that we know all the answers, and we must
beware of dangerous analogies. To say that little brother "has
gone to sleep" could make the child fear going to sleep at night.
Or the child might wonder why little brother does not wake
up. "Grandpa has gone on a long journey to heaven" sounds
like a lovely sentiment, but it is fraught with problems. "When
will he come back? Can we write to him or phone him? Will
our next trip be to heaven? Why did Grandpa go alone? Does
Grandpa still care about us? Why did he go?"

Another dangerous explanation is, "God had some work
for Mommy to do in heaven." Is God's work in heaven more
important than the mother's work in her home on earth? Does
God need her more than her children need her? Could she not
"work for God" just as well on earth? God must be very selfish!

It is usually unwise to emphasize the physical cause of
death, such as sickness or accident. Many people become ill
and do not die. Why did *Daddy* die? Many people experience
automobile accidents and come out unscathed. Why did *big
brother* get killed? To blame death on sickness or accident could
well frighten the child into concluding that the next time he
is sick, he will die; or the next time he rides in a car, he may
be killed.

"Grandma has gone to heaven" maybe is a true statement,
but it can create confusion, because the child knows that
Grandma's body was put into a grave in the cemetery. Older
children may be able to grasp the idea of the person's soul (or
spirit) leaving the body and going to be with Christ, but it is
not likely younger children will. In the Christian home, the
parents can teach their children about heaven through Bible
stories, Sunday school lessons, and daily conversation; and
they may be amazed at the faith and perception of their children.

Perhaps the best analogy is the one Paul uses in 1 Corinthians 15:35-50, the planting of the seed. Children are acquainted with trees and flowers and realize that they grow,
produce fruit and flowers, and then "die," only to reappear in
the spring. This is a law of nature that has been instituted by
God. Our bodies are like seeds. We plant the body in the ground

in the cemetery ("God's acre"), and one day it will be raised in glory and beauty, a new body fitted for eternity.

When a child dies after a long illness, there can be problems with the siblings. For one thing, a sick child usually gets more attention than his brothers and sisters, especially if it is known to be a terminal case. The siblings might resent that, and then feel guilty when the brother or sister dies. It is possible that the siblings envied the sick child and even thought (or said), "I wish he was dead!" When the death does occur, they may blame themselves and feel very guilty.

One funeral director told us that his experience has been that, the greater the age difference between siblings, the greater the difficulty in their adjusting to the death of a brother or sister. Older children who probably helped to care for the younger child would naturally feel the loss more. Likewise, younger children who looked to the older brother or sister for security would feel their loss deeply.

In his post-funeral ministry, the pastor will want to meet the whole family on occasion and see how the members are relating to the loss and to each other. He will certainly have his private times with the parents (or parent), because the parent(s) must be the source of encouragement and growth in the home.

When little Bruce died, the pastor met with the entire family and asked each member, "What is your happiest memory about Bruce?" That opened up a wonderful opportunity for him to learn more about the boy as well as about the family. It also gave the parents and children opportunity to express both joy and sorrow. It was the beginning of the healing process for them.

Should children attend a funeral service? It depends on the age and the comprehension of the child. Certainly the funeral service should be explained to the child so he or she is not surprised at what happens. To insist that a child remain at home is to give the impression that "something is going on" that is very important and very secret; and the child may think, *What are they hiding from me? Am I in danger? Will I die?*

A child must not be forced to attend. If he or she prefers to remain at home, the parents can explain what happened when they return. Perhaps they can visit the grave when the child feels up to it. Each child is different, and each situation is different; but the important thing is that what is done be the very best for the child. The absence of a family member at the funeral need not embarrass anybody. After all, the purpose of the funeral is the healing of the mourners, not the defending of protocol.

The funeral of a child should have its own special atmosphere—tenderness, simplicity, quietness, the soft breath of the nursery, not the strong wind of the lecture room. If there are children present, the pastor must be sure his words will mean something to them. Fortunately, there are many images in the Bible that can be adapted to a funeral message that will have both biblical content and loving intent.

Here are some messages we have used, and some outlines of messages, any of which may be adapted to new situations.

1

When someone comes into your life for only an hour, and wins your heart, and then leaves, how can you describe the feeling down inside? Little Mary was born last Tuesday. After spending an hour with her parents, she slipped into heaven, into the presence of Jesus.

The question that keeps coming to all of us is, "Why?" Why would our loving God invest nine months of precious life in Mary, and then take it away after one short hour in this world? Why?

There is certainly nothing wrong with asking the question "Why?" Many godly people found in the Bible asked, "Why?" including our Lord Jesus Christ. Our Father knows that these painful experiences trouble us, and that we don't always have the faith we need when we need it. That's the reason we keep asking, "Why?"

Well, I must confess that I don't know why, and I doubt if anybody else knows. But this I know: even if we could explain why Mary left us, the explanation wouldn't begin to heal our broken hearts. We don't need reasons today; we need spiritual resources to help us accept this sorrow and be able to go back to life better able to carry the burdens.

There are some truths that we do know for certain, and I want to share them with you. If we will just lay hold of these certainties, our broken hearts will start to mend.

To begin with, we can be sure that *God shares in our sorrow*. The prophet Isaiah wrote, "In all their affliction, He was afflicted" (63:9). Isaiah also called our Lord Jesus "a man of sorrows, and acquainted with grief" (53:3). Jesus wept at the grave of Lazarus. He entered into the sorrows that Mary and Martha were experiencing.

Remember, Jesus loved the little children—and the children loved Him! They loved to be with Him, and He welcomed them. Can you conceive of Jesus being indifferent to the needs of a child? Can't you see Him blessing the children and their parents? We can be sure of one thing today: God knows our heartache.

Remember, too, that our heavenly Father knows what it means to have a child die. "For God so loved the world that He gave His only begotten Son." We don't fully understand all the mysteries of the cross, but this we know: the Father loved His Son—and loves us—and the Father was willing to give His Son that we might be saved. Today, right now, God shares in your sorrows.

There is a second certainty that we must lay hold of: *Mary is with Jesus*. Do you remember what King David said about his own little baby who died? "I shall go to him, but he shall not return to me" [2 Sam. 12:23]. Where was David going? He tells us in Psalm 23—"and I will dwell in the house of the Lord forever" [vs.6]. David knew that he would one day go to heaven and there meet his son.

In days to come, we will talk about the loss of this child; but you don't lose something when you know where it is! Jesus welcomed the little children when He was here on earth, and He welcomes the children home to heaven. And, since heaven is a place of perfection and fulfillment, I believe that our little ones grow up in heaven so that they can enjoy all of its beauty and glory—and that one day they will welcome us when our turn comes to go home.

There will always be a special place in our hearts for Mary. We will sometimes think about what might have been if—! But this we know, we shall see her and be with her when Jesus Christ comes and takes us home.

God shares in our sorrow. Mary is with Jesus Christ. Of this, we can be sure.

The third certainty is this: *God's grace is sufficient for us right now, and it always will be*: "My grace is sufficient for thee" [2 Cor. 12:9]. Grace means God's resources are available to us if only we will trust Him and ask Him. He is "the God of all grace" [1 Pet. 5:10] and "the God of all comfort" [2 Cor. 1:3]. We don't have to earn His grace—all we have to do is accept it and let it work in our lives.

Whenever something precious is taken from us, we feel that nothing is really worthwhile anymore. This is a normal feeling that most people have when death invades the home. But life *is* worth living! God is still in control, and we have nothing to fear. Jesus Christ has conquered death, and He is with us as we go through the valley. We won't stay in the valley forever, because at the end of the valley is the Father's house.

We live a day at a time. We live depending on God's limitless grace. He can fill the empty place in our hearts. He can give us the strength to weep so that our tears are not hopeless. He can equip us to carry the burdens of life. He can strengthen us so we can help others whose hearts are also broken with grief.

Mary had such a short life, yet from it we can learn two very precious lessons. First, let's appreciate the miracle of life. Let's not take it for granted. Life comes from God, and life is sacred. No matter how brief the time span, all life is important to God.

Second, let's take advantage of the time God gives us with our loved ones and friends. I'm sure all of us will appreciate each other more, simply because of Mary's brief visit in our midst. Without saying a word, without staying very long, she preached a great sermon that we must never forget.

"And He took them in His arms and blessed them."

Let Him take you in His strong arms and bless you. He can do it, because He is the "God of all comfort."

2

There is only one place for a little child, and that is in somebody's arms. That is the safest place, the most loving place—in somebody's arms.

When Jesus was here on earth, He welcomed the children into His arms. [Read Mark 10:13-16, using "permit" instead of "suffer," a word that could be misunderstood.]

But Jesus Christ is not on earth! True, but that makes the blessing even greater. Because Jesus is alive in heaven, He is not hampered by the limitations of a humble human body. If He were still on earth, He could not be everywhere at one time—and we would not have His presence with us here today, to give us the strength that we need.

The newspaper article said that Jimmy died, but you and I know better. Jimmy was taken up in the arms of Jesus, the safest place in the world, the most loving place in the world. I know—all of us are saying, "Yes, we believe that, but we'd much rather have Jimmy in *our* arms!" Of course we would! We loved Jimmy, and we wanted him to stay with us longer. But our loving Lord had other plans.

Someone has said that when a soldier dies, we say, "There goes a hero!" But when a child dies, we say, "Something is wrong somewhere." I don't believe it was ever God's plan for children to die like this and for parents and loved ones to suffer. But, we aren't in heaven yet. We must live in a world where sin and death reign, and where the last enemy—death—has not yet been destroyed.

We hurt today because a piece of our lives, a piece of our hearts, and part of our future, has been taken from us. What can we do?

For one thing, we can tell our heavenly Father how much we hurt and ask Him for the help that we need. There is nothing wrong with tears. God made us with the ability to weep, and He expects us to weep. But as Christians, we don't sorrow as those who have no hope. Even in the midst of our sorrow, we can experience the strength and the calmness of God's grace.

We can also tell our heavenly Father that we trust Him,

even though we don't understand. When they arrested Jesus in the Garden, Peter tried to defend Him with a sword. Jesus rebuked Peter and said, "Put up thy sword . . . the cup which my Father hath given me, shall I not drink it?" (John 18:11). Peter tried to fight God's will, but Jesus calmly accepted God's will. What is in *your* hand today—the sword, or the cup? We need never fear any cup that the Father has prepared for us. At the time, it may be bitter; but in the end, it will be sweet.

I wish I could explain why this happened, but I cannot. Nor can you. And, I'm not so sure that explanations are what we need today. I think we need *promises*—promises like [read John 14:1-6 and other great promises].

Jesus loves the children. Jesus welcomes the children and enfolds them in His arms of love. Jesus cares for the children. Their angels behold God's glory at the throne of heaven.

Yes, we wish that Jimmy were in our arms, but he is not. He is in the arms of Jesus. One day, all of us will be together— and then we can put our arms around the Lord and around Jimmy—and then we will understand why it all happened as it did.

Meanwhile, let's keep our arms around one another, loving one another, caring for one another. And let's trust our heavenly Father to carry us through the valley. "The eternal God is thy refuge, and underneath are the everlasting arms" [Deut. 33:27].

3

"Weeping may endure for a night, but joy cometh in the morning" [Psalm 30:5].

That sounds like the normal experience of a child. When night comes, he [she] doesn't want to go to sleep; so he cries. But when morning comes, he bounds out of bed and enters the day joyfully.

As parents, we try to convince the child that he needs the sleep, that weeping isn't necessary. We tell him that the morning will come with all sorts of exciting things to see and do.

Well, now it is we adults who need that sermon! We are

the ones who are weeping! And the Father is trying to console us the way we used to console ——. "Weeping may endure for a night, but joy cometh in the morning."

  I. The night of weeping
     A. Christians do sorrow
     B. Night—nothing looks right
     C. But it is temporary
 II. The morning of joy
     A. Morning does come!
        1. The morning of resurrection when He returns
        2. The morning of victory today, when we trust Him
     B. We shall see things clearly
     C. We shall rejoice eternally

God sees our sorrow now and gently reminds us that joy is coming in the morning.

But for those who don't know Jesus Christ, the joy is now—but the weeping is yet to come!

This precious child was "put to sleep by Jesus," and for us it is a night of weeping. One day the trumpet will sound, and it will be morning! "Weeping may endure for a night, but joy cometh in the morning."

4

"He shall feed his flock like a shepherd: he shall gather the lambs with his arm, and carry them in his bosom, and shall gently lead those that are with young" (Isa. 40:11).

  I. The Good Shepherd guides us
     1. He knows what is best
     2. We need not question His will
 II. The Good Shepherd gathers His sheep
III. The Good Shepherd especially cares for the lambs

5

1 Samuel 1:27-28

   I. We pray for our children
  II. We receive them as God's gifts
 III. We give them back to the Lord
 IV. No matter what He does, we worship Him

12

Suicide

Suicide is a major problem these days, not only in the United States, but in other nations as well. There are at least 27,000 suicides in the United States annually. That figures out to one every twenty minutes. (Some experts estimate that *every minute* there is an attempted suicide in the United States!) At least twenty percent of the suicides are youths between the ages of fifteen and twenty-four. In fact, suicide is the number three killer among these youths, and the number two among college students.

According to Earl A. Grollman, the "typical American suicide" would be a male Protestant Caucasian, in his teens or over sixty-five, living in the city, living alone (single, divorced, widowed), unemployed, and having serious personal problems. Special high risk groups include dentists, doctors, psychiatrists, and lawyers. Protestants have the highest suicide rate, with Roman Catholics second and Jews third. There are more suicides during April and the Christmas season. Starting about two weeks before Christmas, the suicide rate jumps 5 to 10 percent, and the number of attempted suicides jumps 20 to 30 percent.

Social scientists have noted that a front-page suicide story will generate even more suicides. Professor David Phillips of the University of California has proved that within two months after a front-page suicide story, an average of fifty-eight more people than usual will take their lives. There will also be more fatal accidents, including plane accidents. The suicide of a popular entertainer can trigger a host of suicides across the nation.

The modern emphasis on "the right to die" has given suicide an aura of respectability. Instead of being an act of cowardice, it is considered an act of courage. The suicides of famous writers such as Virginia Woolf, Sylvia Plath, and Ernest Hemingway have almost been sanctified by some of their cultic followers.

Our present concern is ministering to the people who are left behind, people who are shocked because of what the loved one did. Perhaps the major problem is *guilt*. In fact, some authorities conclude that guilt is exactly the result the suicide is intended to produce. The person who commits suicide is often angry and disappointed and wants to hurt the people that should have helped him. The suicide victim wants to punish them and is willing to destroy his or her own life in order to accomplish it.

Family members find different ways to deal with their guilt. Some rationalize the suicide by saying that the person was mentally ill or perhaps even demon possessed. If the person was on medication, "He took an accidental overdose." One of the easiest outs is to blame somebody—the psychiatrist, the doctor, the pastoral counselor, the boss who fired him.

Whether we like it or not, there is still a stigma attached to death by suicide. It is sometimes called "the death we whisper about." Many people who commit suicide appear to be successful people, but by taking their own lives, they demonstrate that they were unable to cope and decided to give up.

The sensitive pastor will try to avoid passing judgment or giving simplistic explanations. Dr. Karl Menninger said that "suicide is a very complex act," and so we had better leave the analysis to God. At the same time, the pastor will not try to avoid the fact that a suicide has taken place. It does no good to encourage a fantasy approach to grief, because that will only make things worse. Studies indicate that a suicide leaves behind survivors who experience more depression and physical problems than mourners whose loved ones died natural deaths. In short, it's tough to be a suicide survivor, and the grief work is difficult.

The Bible does not say much about suicide. It records the

suicides of six men: Samson (Judges 16:30); Saul and his armor-bearer (1 Sam. 31:4-5); Ahithophel (2 Sam. 17:23); Zimri (1 Kings 16:18); and Judas (Matt. 27:5). Except for Judas, who "went to his own place" (Acts 1:25), nothing is said about their destiny. Judas went to perdition, not because he committed suicide, but because he did not trust Jesus Christ (John 6:66-71).

Theologians have debated for centuries whether suicides can go to heaven. What the minister believes and preaches depends on his own theological orientation. It is our belief that personal salvation is a completed transaction and that the way a person dies cannot rob him of eternal life. However, regardless of what the minister believes about suicide and salvation, it is not a subject to be brought into a public funeral service. His purpose is not to explain theology but to apply the truth of God to the hearts of people who are shocked, grieved, and feeling very guilty. The preacher must be neither a judge nor a defense attorney; he must be a loving shepherd.

Of course, the two key questions are "Why?" and "Why us?" If we had a faithful transcript of the victim's thoughts and actions, we could probably explain *why*; but that would not really solve any problems. In fact, it could increase guilt as people realized the signals they missed and the warnings they ignored. The patient pastor will have to deal with these matters when he counsels the family privately. If he talks about it at all in the public message, he must be careful to use the pronoun "we" (even if he was not the suicide's pastor), lest he give the impression he is passing judgment on others.

It is not necessary to use the word *suicide* in the public service. "What has happened is a tragedy, and all of us feel it deeply. It should not have happened, and we wish it had not happened. But we cannot change the past. In fact, we may not really understand the past. The important thing is that we learn from this tragic event what we need to know about ourselves, about God, and about life."

Dietrich Bonhoeffer defined suicide as "man's attempt to give a final human meaning to a life which has become humanly meaningless." In the funeral message, the pastor must be an interpreter who can give insight and meaning to a difficult situation, even though he cannot fully explain what happened or why it happened.

King David has set a good example for all of us to follow. In his "Song of the Bow" (2 Sam. 1:17-27), he had only *good* things to say about Saul, a man who was guilty of many crimes, including suicide. The funeral message ought to focus on the good aspects of the person's life, the things worth remembering. The fact that he or she ended life in a tragic manner need not detract from the lasting contributions made during that life.

In short, the entire service should be positive, and it should be introduced in that way. The minister might open with: "Blessed are the merciful, for they shall obtain mercy. Thou, Lord, art good, and ready to forgive; and plenteous in mercy unto all them that call upon thee. Thou, O Lord, art a God full of compassion, and gracious, longsuffering, and plenteous in mercy and truth. [Ps. 86:5, 15]"

In his pastoral prayer, he can voice the concern of the loved ones without going into embarrassing details. "Father, forgive us for the things we have not done that we should have done. We have not always been as concerned as we should be, as alert to the needs of others. But we would ask for more than forgiveness. We would ask for a more loving and sensitive spirit, so that we might help others bear the burdens of life. You cannot change the past, but You can help us be more Christlike as we face the future."

One further word: the pastor should carefully read every verse of the songs that will be sung, lest there be some line or phrase that would create embarrassment at the funeral of a suicide. He should examine his own Scripture selections just as carefully. Since all of us have a tendency to repeat set phrases in our prayers, he must be cautious not to say anything embarrassing. To open the prayer with "We thank Thee that——is home with the Lord" is tantamount to approving the suicide!

1

Text: Romans 8:38-39

Message given at the funeral of a young man who took an overdose of drugs. The cause of his death was not widely known, but enough people knew it that the minister had to take it into consideration.

We are here today because of love, our love for Larry, and God's love for us and for him. It's because we loved Larry so deeply that his absence makes us hurt so much down inside. Death is something that separates us. We are separated from Larry, and we feel as though a part of us has been amputated.

But Paul's words tell us that there is one thing from which death can never separate us, and that is the love of God. "For I am persuaded that neither life nor death . . . can separate us from the love of God, which is in Christ Jesus our Lord."

Larry had experienced the love of Christ in his heart. When he was ten years old, he trusted Christ as his Savior at a Sunday school meeting. We believe that today, Larry is in heaven with the Savior, because absolutely nothing can separate us from God's love.

But what kind of love is the love of God?

To begin with, it is *a love that seeks*. We may not like the comparison, but the Bible tells us that all of us are like sheep. We are prone to wander. "All we like sheep have gone astray." Jesus Christ is the Good Shepherd Who seeks the lost sheep and brings it back to the fold. "My sheep hear my voice," said Jesus, " . . . and I give unto them eternal life, and they shall never perish."

You see, God in His love accepts us for who we are. We don't have to improve ourselves for God to love us or receive us. Larry often struggled with this matter of acceptance. There were days when he had a hard time accepting himself, and sometimes he felt as though others had rejected him. But of this he was sure: Christ in His love and grace had received him and accepted him.

Yes, God's love is a love that seeks—and once the Good Shepherd finds us, He never loses us.

But God's love is also *a love that saves*. "For the Son of man is come to seek and to save that which was lost" [Luke 19:10]. John 3:16 is a familiar verse, but it says what needs to be said.

What kind of love is the love of God in Jesus Christ? It is a love that seeks and a love that saves. But it is also *a love that keeps*. Listen to Paul's wonderful words of assurance [Rom. 8:38-39].

This is an exciting truth: nothing can separate us from God's love! No matter how difficult the circumstances may be, God's love is still there. What people are and what they do cannot separate us from God's love. Even the very demons from hell and the angels from heaven are helpless to isolate us from God's great love. Nothing in life and nothing in death can come between us and the love of God.

God never turns His back on His children. God never adjusts His love to their conduct. His love is an everlasting love, and a love that never changes, a love that keeps us. Those of you who knew Larry know that there were times when he felt as though his friends had let him down. He was sometimes hurt by things that they did and said. But he could be sure that his Father in heaven would never let him down—or let him go! When the Good Shepherd gives His life for His sheep, He makes sure that they are secure.

Finally, God's love in Jesus Christ is *a love that unites*. Death brings physical separation, and with that separation comes heartache. We sorrow, but not as those who have no hope. Where there is love, there is always hope.

One day, Jesus Christ will unite His people and there will be a great reunion. [Read 1 Thess. 4:13-18.] Jesus called heaven "My Father's house." Heaven is a home, and that means love. Larry cannot return to us, but one day we shall go to him. Meanwhile, he is enjoying God's love, and we are experiencing God's love, and that links our hearts together until we meet again.

This tragedy is something we cannot explain or fully understand. But broken hearts are not healed by explanations— they are healed by love and the grace of God. Jesus died and rose again so that you and I might receive God's forgiveness, enter God's family, and experience God's love—a love that seeks, saves, keeps, and unites. Have you experienced the love of God?

"For I am persuaded, that neither death, nor life, nor angels, nor principalities, nor powers, nor things present, nor things to come, nor height, nor depth, nor any other creature, shall be able to separate us from the love of God, which is in Christ Jesus our Lord."

2

"Lord, if—" [John 11:21, 32].

"Lord, if—." Two little words that today touch us where

we really are. "Lord, if—." Martha said it to Jesus, and Mary
said it to Jesus; and you and I have been saying it either to
ourselves or to the Lord for the past few days. "Lord, if—."

Two little words. One of them hurts, and the other one
heals. *If* is the word that hurts, but *Lord* is the word that heals.

Let's start with "if"—the word that hurts.

If Brian had not been left alone. *If* one of us had caught
the signals and acted promptly. *If* somehow our plans that day
could have been different. *If* one of his friends had stopped by
to see him or even telephoned him. If —!

If is the word that hurts. Do you know why it hurts? Because *if* looks back to a past that cannot be changed. *If* looks
back and raises a host of questions that nobody can answer. *If*
is not a word that encourages faith, because *if* looks backward,
whereas faith looks forward. What we need today is faith to
believe that God is in control, that He is working all things
together for good, even though we don't understand the plan
that He has.

There is another reason why *if* hurts: *if* is a word that asks
for explanations, and life doesn't always furnish explanations.
Why did this happen? is the question in everybody's heart. But
we will never fully understand why until we get to heaven and
see the total picture. Even if we did have a full explanation
today, it wouldn't bring Brian back to us, and it wouldn't heal
our aching hearts.

If hurts us because *if* is actually a selfish word, and selfishness is the last thing we need today. When we start talking
about all the *ifs* in this experience, we are suggesting that perhaps God doesn't know what He is doing. Don't misunderstand
me—I'm not saying that our heavenly Father is responsible for
all the decisions that His children make. But I am saying that
God is still on the throne and that He knows what has happened
and how we feel today.

I suppose in the final analysis, *if* is a word that hurts because *if* can be very selfish. It can smack of pride. You and I
are suggesting that *we* know what is best, that if *we* had been
consulted, things would have been different. *If* becomes a mir-
ror in which we see ourselves, when what we need is a window
through which we can see God.

If is a normal word for us to use in a difficult experience like
this. But we must recognize the fact that *if* is the word that hurts.

However, *Lord* is the word that heals! When you and I come to Jesus Christ and say, "Lord!" then the healing will begin in our hearts. Mary and Martha were brokenhearted. Their brother had died, and Jesus apparently had done nothing to prevent his death. By the time Jesus arrived at the grave of Lazarus, the man had been dead four days!

But both Mary and Martha were able to say, "Lord!" What kind of a Lord is He? Why is it that "Lord" is the word that heals?

For one thing, Jesus Christ is *the Lord of love*, and love always heals. "Lord, behold, he whom thou lovest is sick" [v. 3]. "Now Jesus loved Martha, and her sister, and Lazarus" [v. 5]. "Behold, how he loved him!" [v. 36]. The tragedy of Lazarus's death did not change the fact that Jesus loved him and his sisters.

In love, Jesus came to them in their hour of need, just as He comes to us today. In love, He spoke words of encouragement, just as He speaks to us from His Word today. In love, He wept; and right now our Lord feels the pain in our hearts and enters into our sorrows. But the greatest proof of the love of God is not Jesus at the grave, or Jesus weeping, but Jesus on the cross. "But God commendeth his love toward us, in that, while we were yet sinners, Christ died for us" [Rom. 5:8].

He is the Lord of love, and He is *the Lord of life*. "I am the resurrection and the life!" Martha believed in the resurrection, but she saw it only as a future event. Jesus said that resurrection is a present experience. Those who have trusted Jesus Christ can experience resurrection power in their lives today! The power of His resurrection is what will carry us through.

Jesus Christ is *the Lord of glory*. The emphasis in this chapter is on the glory of God [vv. 4, 40]. We can't change the past, but the way we use the past can help us in the future. God can take even the seeming tragedies of life and work them out for our good and His glory. The way we weep, the way we encourage each other, the way we carry our burdens—all of these can be used to the glory of God.

For the Christian, the best is yet to come. Death is only sleep, according to the Lord. The spirit goes home to be with Christ, but the body sleeps, awaiting resurrection morning. If death is sleep, then there is nothing to fear. Jesus Christ has taken the sting out of death, and we share His resurrection victory.

Here, then, are two little words that you and I must understand and deal with—"Lord, if—." *If* is the word that hurts, but *Lord* is the word that heals.

We are Christians. We don't want to say "Lord, if —."

We simply want to say, *Lord*!

3

Text: 1 Corinthians 13:11-13

Paul describes two opposite attitudes toward life:

(1) *The child*—everything must be explained;

(2) *The adult*—willing to accept mysteries, darkness, problems.

We must be mature as we face life and death, especially when we face the tragedies of life.

Two little words help us to understand and accept what has happened, and use it to the glory of God.

I. *Now*
   A. We wish that "now" were different
   B. We can't see, but God can
   C. We know He loves us and cares
II. *Then*
   A. There is a "then"—a hereafter
   B. Christians have a bright future!
      1. From the partial to the perfect
      2. From the temporary to the eternal
      3. From vague reflections to full recognition

We have *faith*—that takes care of the unexplained mysteries.

We have *hope*—that heals the wounds of disappointment.

We have *love*—that overcomes loneliness and emptiness.

Not now, but in the coming years,
It may be in a better land;
We'll read the meaning of our tears,
And there, sometime we'll understand.

God knows the way, He holds the key,
He guides us with unerring hand;
Sometime with tearless eyes we'll see,
Yes, there—up there, we'll understand.

Then trust in God through all the days,
Fear not, for He doth hold thy hand.
Though dark thy way, still sing and praise,
Sometime, sometime we'll understand.

Maxwell N. Cornelius

13

The Murder Victim

There was a time when the average minister rarely had a funeral service where the deceased was the victim of foul play. But in these days of violence, it is not unusual for a church family to lose a loved one because of murder, and that includes children. The loving pastor must deal with people who are shocked that God would permit such a thing to happen, and perplexed that it should happen to them.

The funeral service is not the place for a theological discussion of the providence of God or the vexing problem of evil in this world. We live in a world in which tragedies abound, everything from plane crashes and earthquakes to famines and murders; and the wise pastor will deal with these things in the regular course of his pulpit ministry. Every congregation needs to be taught what the Bible says about both natural and moral evil, and how the Christian message can bring hope and healing.

One of the few times Jesus discussed the theme of human tragedy is recorded in Luke 13:1-9. He made no attempt to explain why the Lord permitted Pilate to kill those Jews, or why that tower was allowed to fall on those eighteen men. He made it clear that we are not to pass judgment on those who died ("They must have been evil people to experience such a thing!") but to examine our own hearts. We must not blame

God or the victims. In the parable that followed, Jesus taught that the most important question is not "Why did *they* die?" but "Why am *I* still alive? Is there any good reason God should permit me to live?"

We have used this text and approach at funerals conducted for victims of foul play, and we have found that it ministers to needs. Instead of trying to explain why the victim died, we have emphasized the importance of making good use of the lives God has given us. Even if the victim is to blame, the principle still applies: we cannot change the past, but we can make better use of the present and future. We never know when God may order our "tree" to be cut down!

From the divine viewpoint, our Savior's death was voluntary; He willingly laid down His life. But from the human point of view, He was taken by wicked hands and slain (Acts 2:23, 3:15). Our Lord knows what it means to be handled violently and then killed. He is able to sympathize with those whose loved ones have experienced such a violent death.

How a person dies is not as important as where he goes after he dies. However, in saying this, the pastor must not give the appearance that he is minimizing the horror of the death. No mother or father wants a child to be abused and murdered. No husband or wife wants to think about his or her mate's dying at the hand of a fiend. Death itself is bad enough; when death is mingled with the dark shadows of violence and crime, it is even worse.

Of course, there is always the desire for vengeance, especially if the criminal has not been caught. In such situations, Christians sometimes find it difficult to separate official justice and personal revenge. Romans 12:19-20 certainly applies. Not to have a forgiving spirit only makes the pain worse and the healing more difficult. "Father, forgive them; for they know not what they do" is a powerful text that reveals the ignorance of the offender and the willingness of God to forgive.

Many texts in the Bible make it clear that we live in a sinful society and that even innocent Christians can be victims of tragedy. Solomon pondered this problem (Eccles. 3:16-17 and 4:1), and even the parable of the Good Samaritan touches upon it (Luke 10:25-37).

Psalm 11 is David's expression of confidence in God that,

even though the wicked seem to prosper, one day God will make all things right. This is a vivid chapter with pictures of a bird flying away to shelter, an enemy aiming his bow, the foundations shaking, and God in His holy temple in complete control. We feel like running away from it all, but where shall we run? It seems that justice is vanished, but God is still on the throne. In many of the psalms, the writer wrestles with the age-old problem of why the righteous suffer and the wicked seem to escape (see Ps. 73, for example).

Another approach is to emphasize the suddenness of death, which is often the case when there is a murder. First Samuel 20:3 is applicable here, when David confessed, "There is but a step between me and death." David's statement reveals that death is certain, can be sudden, and when it comes, it is final. But there is also a step between us and *life*—the step of faith in Jesus Christ. We live on the brink of eternity, and it behooves us to be ready when death comes.

At the funeral of a murder victim, there is no reason to relate the painful details or to use the service as an opportunity to condemn either society or our judicial system. What people need is a message that comes to grips with the facts of life and death, but that also relates them to the eternal. The minister who knows his Bible—especially the Psalms—will find texts that will shine with new meaning as he walks through the valley with the bereaved family.

14

Multiple Deaths

One of the earliest funerals we conducted was for a young mother and her four-year-old daughter, both of whom died when the stove exploded in the kitchen. Multiple deaths are often connected with tragedy—an auto accident, a murder and suicide, a fire, or some onslaught of nature (earthquake, flood, wind). When the deceased are the mother and father, and only the children are left, it is not easy to know what to say.

Once again, the minister must help the people face the reality of it and feel the enormity of it, but also recognize the sovereignty of God and the availability of His sustaining grace. Psalm 27 has been a strengthening Word for many in these difficult situations, and so has Psalm 37. Of course, the wise pastor will select from these psalms those verses that best meet the immediate needs.

When a Christian husband and wife were both killed in an auto accident, someone remarked at the funeral, "Well, they always did everything together. It's only right that they should go home together." "Together with the Lord" would be an appropriate theme (1 Thess. 4:13-18). Another appropriate text would be Ruth's great confession of love and devotion (Ruth 1:16-17).

15

The "Wicked Sinner"

During the Victorian Era in England, a man named John H. Starkey murdered his wife. He was tried and executed, and the authorities asked General William Booth, founder of the Salvation Army, to preach the funeral sermon. Booth faced that day a congregation of hard-hearted sinners who had little regard for either God or man. He opened the sermon with this arresting statement: "John H. Starkey did not have a praying mother!" Many of the men in the congregation *did* have praying mothers, and the statement hit home.

We are not likely to confront that kind of congregation, but we can learn from Booth's strategy. There is no sense trying to preach an ungodly man into heaven (although nobody knows what eternal transactions may have been made before the man died); but it does make good sense to sound a positive note and hope to get an echo from the hearts of the listeners.

Who is this "wicked man" whose funeral we are conducting? He may be a drunkard, a gambler, a notorious derelict, a man given to profanity and defiance of God. Whatever he is, everybody knows about it, and many people will come to the service wondering, *What will the preacher say?* He might also be the husband or father of a godly member of the church. We recall one such husband's telling us, "If the floor opened up and I dropped right into hell, it wouldn't bother me one bit!"

Fortunately, that man trusted Christ before he died; and the minister who conducted the service had joyful news to report.

And we might as well face the fact that the "wicked sinner" could well be a woman. But, whether man or woman, even the "wicked sinner" deserves a decent burial in spite of the fact that a Christian funeral cannot change the past.

Jesus was the friend of publicans and sinners (Matt. 11:19; Luke 15:1-2). When His enemies accused Him, His reply was a series of beautiful parables that reveal the value of the individual soul to God and the willingness of the Father to receive and forgive (Luke 15). The first thing the pastor wants to do is make sure his own heart is tender and forgiving. Certainly the friends and family have had enough burdens and heartaches while the loved one lived. Why should God's witness become a prosecuting attorney and make the burden greater?

That does not mean that the minister whitewashes the past or brightens the future of a profligate sinner. But it does mean that he ministers in love to the people who are there, and that he shows them the grace of God available for their own lives. A false hope is a broken reed and can never bear the burden. God's truth is a strong tower and provides ample refuge for the brokenhearted.

Psalm 81 may be just the medicine needed. In the first ten verses, the writer talks about God's goodness to Israel, how He gave them everything they needed. But in verses 11-12, he laments that the people rejected God's blessing and went their own way. The psalm closes with the writer weeping over the things that might have been. God permits us to have our own way, but only after He has exhausted the influences of His love and grace. Oh, how much we miss when we leave God's will out of our lives! The things that might have been *can still be—* for those who can yet repent and trust Christ.

Texts like Matthew 8:11-12 and 25:31-46 suggest that there will be some surprises at the judgment. Self-satisfied religious sinners (and every church has them) will have a greater judgment than the open sinners. Simon the Pharisee certainly was wrong in his estimate of both the weeping woman and the loving Savior (Luke 7:36-50). There are in our society prodigal sons who are wasteful and wicked, and also elder brothers who are self-righteous and critical. We must avoid both extremes.

Again, the important thing is not to pass judgment on the dead, but to press the claims of Christ on the living. The first few sentences of the message should set the tone and capture their interest, just as William Booth did in his message.

Finally, there is usually something good that can be said about any person. Although a man's goodness will never get him into heaven, certainly it ought not to be forgotten on earth. We recall one profligate who, in spite of his sins and selfishness, was very kind to the children in his neighborhood. He was a bad example but a kind neighbor. This well-known fact was mentioned at the funeral, not to justify his sins, but to introduce the theme: the Christ who loved the children and welcomed them. "Except you repent and become as little children" was the logical conclusion of the message.

We must never forget the thief on the cross (Luke 23:39-43). He is often used as an encouraging example of a deathbed conversion, but certainly much more is involved. Instead of seizing his *last* opportunity to be saved, perhaps it was his *first* opportunity! And think of the courage needed to confess Christ openly before that derisive mob. However one interprets the passage, one thing is clear: where there is life, there is hope. We never know what transpires between the soul and God as that soul is about to enter eternity. The pastor must be careful not to handle this text in such a way that careless sinners will take it as a *guarantee* of a last-minute opportunity. No guarantee is there. Nor should the minister suppose that something happened between the sinner and God. Only God knows. However, the passage is rich with truths that can warn the sinner and encourage the brokenhearted.

Sometimes at the funeral of a "wicked sinner," the atmosphere is just right for a loving but plain-spoken message on sin and salvation. The minister must be careful, however, not to take advantage of the situation and deliberately alienate people who desperately need to be reached. But when a beloved shepherd speaks the truth in love, God will bless and hearts will be opened. A familiar verse like John 3:16 can become a moving funeral text. So can John 11:35—"Jesus wept." If our Lord wept over a good man who died and went to heaven, how much more would He weep over a bad man who died and went to hell? (Again, the minister must not pass judgment; but he should not be afraid to state facts.)

Although sentimentality ought to be avoided at funeral services, there is certainly a place for true sentiment—home, family, mother and father, friendship. The wise pastor will take advantage of those basic human emotions and use them as hinges for opening the door of gospel truth to hearts and minds that otherwise might be closed. If he prepares himself and the message carefully, he will get the seed into their hearts before they know what has happened!

16

The Stranger

Especially in metropolitan areas, the local pastor often finds himself conducting funeral services for people who are strangers to him and to his church. Often, funeral directors are asked to recommend a pastor; and if they find men who are cooperative, they keep them on the list. Perhaps the only reason one pastor is selected rather than another is because the deceased has (or had) a relative who belonged to that pastor's denomination.

The busy pastor must not consider these invitations as interruptions, however. They may be golden opportunities to minister to some new people. We have seen God touch the lives of people through services conducted for total strangers, even when few people have attended.

As with all funeral services, the minister must get as much information as he can; and he must be sure it is accurate. The focus of his message must not be on the fact that the deceased is a stranger to him, or to the church. To open a service with, "I have never met Mr. Jones, and I know little about him" is to ask the congregation to stop listening. On the other hand, to give the impression that you and the deceased were friends would be deceitful. If the deceased was not a churchgoing person, the assembled friends and relatives know that the pastor is there simply by invitation, to maintain tradition.

If possible, the minister should attend the visitation before the funeral and there get acquainted with the friends and family. He can "test the spirits" at that time and get some indication of the direction the service ought to take. Is the group sympathetic to the church and the gospel? Do they consider the pastor an intruder? Are they worldly people with little or no spiritual values, or do they have an interest in spiritual things? Are any of them converted? These are questions the minister should seek to answer before he prepares the service.

Of course, he will want to ask whoever is in charge just what kind of a service is desired. Most likely, the reply will be, "Just do whatever is supposed to be done—and keep it short!" Too often, the deceased stranger has but a few friends and no family (until the will is read!), and those attending the service are there only out of respectful obligation. However, the loving shepherd will do his utmost to serve the people and glorify the Lord. It may well be the only opportunity some of his listeners will have to hear the gospel in a clear and personal way.

In many respects, the unchurched "stranger" and the "wicked sinner" have much in common, so that what we said in the previous section may well be applied here. The deceased will not be unknown to the Lord, even though the minister may not know him; and it is before the Lord that he stands or falls. Andrew Blackwood's counsel applies at this point: do not discuss ethics or eschatology. Preach the gospel, and seek to love the people through the Word.

17

Death in Another Congregation

There was a time when congregations were loyal to their pastor and church family, and when pastors had a sense of ethics and would not "steal sheep" or conduct funerals for members of another church, unless the pastor requested it. Times have changed. Every minister has wept over "church tramps" who run from church to church, following this "great preacher" and worshiping that "deep expositor."

It is our conviction that no minister of the gospel should conduct the funeral service for someone who is not a part of his church family, unless the pastor of the deceased person's church knows about it and approves. When the minister is contacted, either by the family or the funeral director, he should ask where the deceased attended church. If he was a member in good standing of another church, the minister should contact that pastor and discuss the matter with him.

Sometimes church members have fallen out with the pastor and have been looking for another church. No minister should get involved in matters that belong to other congregations, except to pray for God's help for both pastor and people. And the pastor must be careful that the deceased has not been the culprit and perhaps even under discipline.

Whenever we have been asked to conduct a service for someone belonging to another church in the area, we have suggested that the other pastor be included in the service. If the family has rejected the idea, we have asked their permission at least to talk to the other pastor and explain the situation. No minister of the gospel wants to get the reputation of being either a "sheep stealer" or an "ambulance chaser." Men of God who minister in the same area must love and respect one another, even if they differ in matters of theology and fellowship.

When ministers are planning to be out of town, for vacation or the annual conference, they usually contact a friend and ask him to cover for them while they are gone. This is an entirely different matter.

There is one other situation that can be touchy. Suppose the deceased was a member of a cult or a church that rejected the deity of Christ and the message of the gospel? The evangelical minister wants to be very careful lest he compromise his witness. We have never felt it necessary to ask a cult leader or a liberal minister to share the service, but we have felt it the ethical thing to contact them about the funeral and let them know the plans. If a minister has been in a locality long enough, people get to know his position anyway and either accept it or reject it. Again, it is a case of being wise as a serpent but harmless as the dove.

If a family has become dissatisfied with a liberal church, or a cult, and has been shopping around for a new place of worship, and if they request a fundamental minister to conduct the service, there is nothing he can do but cooperate. But he must make clear to their former pastor that he is doing it at their request. This can well be an opportunity to share the truth and win the lost. In personal ministry after the service, the sensitive minister can gently lead the people into the way of truth.

18

Calendar Complications

Death is never convenient and never consults our calendar. When a funeral is conducted near or on a special occasion, it can create either problems or opportunities. Birthdays and wedding anniversaries are especially difficult for the family, and Christmas is almost as difficult.

John 16:20-22 makes a good text for a funeral message when the service is on or near the birthday of the deceased. Our Lord used birth to teach about His own death in particular, but also death in general. Some points to consider are these:

1. Birth is a natural event, and so is death.
2. We prepare for the birth of a baby, and we should prepare for death. Also, the Savior in heaven prepares for the safe arrival of His child (John 14).
3. Birth involves pain, and so does death; but it is we who survive who feel the pain. The deceased believer has entered into eternal joy.
4. Birth brings the baby into a new world, and death ushers the Christian into the new world of glory.

One of the points our Lord was making was this: the same baby that caused the pain for the mother, also caused the joy! Death causes pain for us today, but it means joy tomorrow.

"Weeping may endure for a night, but joy cometh in the morning" (Ps. 30:5).

The Christmas season is an especially hard time for bereaved people. The season is usually marked by joy, but the death of a loved one brings a shadow over the glory of the season. In fact, for years to come, that shadow may remain.

But the angelic Christmas message (Luke 2:8-14) is just what sorrowing hearts need to hear: light in darkness, joy in sorrow, peace in the midst of fear! The reason? A Savior!

We have also used "the tears of Christmas" as a meaningful message (Matt. 2:16-18). There is no time to develop the complex historical background (Jer. 31:15-17), but the pastor should have it in mind. The death of the Bethlehem children certainly illustrates the sorrow that sin has brought into this world. But we do not remember Bethlehem as a place of death; because of Jesus Christ, we remember it as a place of birth. What an opportunity to proclaim the joy and hope of salvation! This is an especially good text for the Christmas season funeral of a baby or child.

A related text (and really a part of the greater context) is Genesis 35:16-20, the birth of Benjamin and the death of Rachel. Again, there was sorrow at Bethlehem, as Rachel the mother died. In her unbelief, she gave her son the wrong name—"son of my sorrow." In faith, Jacob gave the boy a new name—"son of my right hand." (The right hand is the place of power, authority, and honor.) In our time of sorrow, we need the same kind of faith that Jacob displayed. God is at work! He will bring blessing out of tears and triumph out of seeming defeat. For years, the Jews remembered Bethlehem as a *burying* place, but Jesus Christ transformed it into a *birthplace*. At Christmas, even in the midst of sorrow, we must focus on birth, not death.

At the New Year's season, an ideal text is Revelation 21:1-6, emphasizing especially, "Behold, I make all things new!" Death is as old as the human race, but Christ brought newness of life. The best is yet to come!

During the Easter season, any of the great texts that emphasize our Lord's resurrection will certainly be proper. A funeral on Good Friday ("God's Friday") invites the pastor to use one of the great passages from the gospels about the crucifixion of our Lord. How did He face death? Three facts emerge: (1) He surrendered to death; (2) He understands death and therefore can sympathize with us; (3) He conquered death. We have used some of the "words from the cross" as fitting texts for Good Friday funerals, especially Luke 23:46. That seventh cry from the cross indicates that Jesus died confidently, willingly, and victoriously. The quotation is from Psalm 31:5, which was used as a Jewish child's bedtime prayer, not unlike our "Now I lay me down to sleep."

If the deceased was a mother, then the third word from the cross might be appropriate, showing our Lord's love for His mother and His provision for her (John 19:23-27). If you are burying a son, and the grieving mother is present, the text also applies. With spiritual insight and imagination, the creative pastor may take advantage of the special day as he ministers the Word of God.

A Thanksgiving-time funeral suggests the harvest season and Paul's illustration of "Christ . . . the firstfruits" (1 Cor. 15:20-23). The pastor need not give a complicated lecture on the Jewish feasts of Leviticus 23 in order to make the image clear. In a few sentences he can explain what the priest did on the day following Sabbath after Passover and show that this feast anticipated the resurrection of Jesus Christ. The fact that the sheaf is identical to the harvest indicates that we shall one day be like Christ (Phil. 3:20-21; 1 John 3:1-3).

Another great Thanksgiving text is 1 Corinthians 15:57-58. The praise proclaimed in Psalm 103 can also be used to heal broken hearts. "Like as a father pitieth his children, so the Lord pitieth them that fear him" (v.13). What a text! What a Father!

It rarely happens, but the minister may find himself conducting a funeral and a wedding during the same week for the same family. We have had occasion to shepherd the same family through the valley in the morning (the funeral was for the groom's father) and then to the mountaintop of joy in the evening. Circumstances were such that it was impossible to cancel the wedding or change the date and time for the funeral. Wisely, the family canceled the reception after the wedding.

It is in situations such as this that the loving shepherd truly learns to "rejoice with them that do rejoice, and weep with them that weep" (Rom. 12:15). It is only by the grace of

God that His people can experience such conflicting emotions and still maintain their joy and balance. In fact, Romans 12:15 would be a good text for such occasions. The minister can point out that our Lord's first public miracle was at a wedding (John 2), and His last after a funeral (John 11). He has entered into all of the experiences of life and is able to sympathize with us.

Another vivid text is Revelation 19:1-9, the great "Hallelujah Chorus" at the marriage of the Lamb.

There may be times when a family will have two funerals very close to each other. They hardly begin to recover from one sorrow when another one hits them. This often occurs when there has been an auto accident, taking one life and leaving others seriously injured. It also occurs with elderly people: the wife will die and the husband may have a heart attack or stroke some weeks later.

The minister must not assume that the experience of the first bereavement has prepared the family for the second. It may turn out to be just the opposite: the second bereavement may undo whatever good was accomplished at the first funeral. When wounds are opened a second time, they hurt even more.

One illuminating text for such funerals is 2 Corinthians 4:6-18. The pastor will not expound the entire passage, of course, but will simply make clear the glorious assurances that the Christian has, even when life and death are attacking him from all sides. What an opportunity to share eternal certainties of the Christian faith! Through Christ, trouble brings triumph, death brings life, and suffering brings glory! Hallelujah, what a Savior!

19

A Member of the Minister's Family

It is not likely that the minister will conduct the service for his own wife or child, although it has been done; but often the minister will conduct the service for his mother or father, a brother or sister, or an in-law. He must be certain that he is up to it before he agrees to serve; and it would not be a bad idea to share the service with another pastor, just in case (at the last minute) he is unable to go through with it.

When a pastor buries a family member, he must keep in mind that he is representing God first, and then the family. He must also keep in mind that others are present who do not belong to the family. A funeral service is usually not the best place for intimate memories or sentimental stories. Certainly it is not the place for dealing with family feuds or other problems. Finally, the minister must be careful how he addresses any unconverted who may be in the family. He must not take advantage of the pulpit either to embarrass them or put on pressure. If his own witness to them has been faithful, he need not force them into a "guilt trip" to get a decision for Christ.

When the minister is a member of the family of the deceased, sometimes other family members may participate by reading the Scriptures (always prepared in advance), leading in prayer, or even sharing an informal obituary. Each family must make its own decision in these matters; and certainly no one should be involved in the service who ought to be sitting in the pew and grieving. Not everybody is able to mourn and minister at the same time.

20

Divided Families

Sometimes the minister will discover that a house is divided, with some of the family members present belonging to a different faith. He will certainly not deliberately offend these people, but neither will he compromise the faith once delivered to the saints.

We have sometimes opened such services with these words:

"Death has come into our midst, into your family. Death is the great leveler—it respects no age, or occupation, or income, or religion. There is no such thing as Protestant death, or Roman Catholic death, or Jewish death. Death is an enemy to all of us. 'It is appointed unto men once to die,' says the Bible. That includes all of us.

"But we have more in common than the experience of death. We all are made in the image of God. We share a common birth and a common blood. We also share a common need for forgiveness, for comfort, for assurance when life ends."

The minister may then move into his text and sermon.

Sometimes the division is not religious but legal: there has been a divorce, perhaps two or three. We recall one service where three different sets of wives and children came to pay respects to the deceased husband and father. The big question at such funerals is not, "Whose husband will he be in the res-

urrection?" but, "What can we say that will lead these needy
people to Jesus Christ?"

Perhaps the approach suggested above can be adapted to
this complicated situation. For example:

"We have been summoned together today, not by life, but
by death. In life, there was division; but today, there is a one-
ness. Why? Because all of us know that death is the lot of all
men and women. We are here today, not because of our dif-
ferences, but because we have one thing in common: 'It is appointed unto men once to die, and after this the judgment.'"

It is best not to refer to family members or any of the events
of the past. The minister must seek to fix their attention on the
God of all grace and pray that they will trust Him.

21
Additional Outlines

1. For Someone Who Died Alone

It grieves our hearts to think that —— died alone, yet, in reality, he (she) was not alone. Consider these four comforts for the Christian from the Word of God.

I. Christ was with him (her) (Ps. 23:4)
II. He (She) is with Christ (2 Cor. 5:8-9)
III. Christ is now with us (Isa. 41:10)
IV. One day, we shall all be together (1 Thess. 4:13-18)

2. The Death of a "Senior Saint"

We thank God for His "senior saints," older people who have lived a long time and been a testimony for the Lord. Simeon was that kind of person (Luke 2:25-32).
Consider the death of one of God's older saints:

I. Planned by God
A. "Now lettest thou . . . "——
B. Depart—a ship setting sail, a soldier taking down a tent

II. Peaceful
   A. He had seen Christ—salvation from God!
   B. He had served God
III. Praise to God
   A. Ready and willing to go—no regrets
   B. Sorrow for us, joys for them

3. For Another Senior Saint (Luke 2:25-32)

Look at him—an old man in the Temple! But he's different from the other old people in the congregation.

I. Look at his eyes—expecting God's promise
   A. Most old people look back, not ahead
   B. Waiting for God's time
   C. Watching for God's salvation
II. Look at his lips—expressing God's praise
   A. An old man singing
   B. The Sovereign Lord in control
   C. The Lord who keeps His promises
III. Look at his heart—experiencing God's peace
   A. Many old people have heart trouble
   B. This word *departure* carries some beautiful meanings
      to the Christian
      1. The releasing of a prisoner
      2. The setting sail of a ship
      3. Taking down the tent to move on
      4. Unyoking a beast of burden

4. Victory over Death (a general message)

Death is a true enemy, yet this enemy has been defeated by Jesus Christ. We know that when a Christian dies, he (she) goes to heaven.

I. Because of the price that Jesus paid (1 Thess. 5:9-10)
II. Because of the promise that Jesus made (John 14:1-6)
III. Because of the prayer that Jesus prayed (John 17:24)

5. Another General Message

We are here today to say good-bye. Jesus knew what this experience was like. [Read John 14:1-6.] Jesus comforted His disciples—and He comforts us—by sharing four truths.

 I. Death is real
   A. We must face it honestly
   B. When we accept it, healing begins
   C. Death to us means glory to [the deceased]
 II. Heaven is real
   A. A real place
   B. A prepared place
   C. A perfect place—home with the Father
 III. Salvation is real
   A. Christ the only way to heaven
   B. Faith the only way to be saved
 IV. Christ's coming is real
   A. It means resurrection
   B. It means reunion
   C. It means comfort today—glory tomorrow

6. For a Sunday School Teacher

Read Luke 10:38-42.
Life is made up of choices, and these choices determine our character and our destiny. Mary chose the "good part."

 I. She chose Christ
 II. She chose His Word
   A. The Word brings salvation (John 5:24)
   B. The Word gives daily strength
   C. The Word gives assurance for life and death
   D. The Word comforts us today

—— has been taken from us. But what she chose can never be taken from her.

7. For One Who Served Faithfully

Text: Acts 13:36.
God sees us as individuals, what we are and what we do.
In David, we see the example of the ideal believer.

  I. In life, he serves
    A. Christ was a servant (Phil. 2)
    B. We serve in many ways
       [Explain the service the deceased rendered]
    C. This is service that counts
      1. In our generation today
      2. Eternally (1 John 2:17)
 II. In death, he sleeps
    A. The body sleeps—applied to believers
       (John 11:11; 1 Thess. 4:13-18)
    B. Why death is compared to sleep
      1. Rest from labor
      2. Harmless—we don't fear sleep
      3. Brief—"for a night" (Ps. 30:5)
      4. Awaken for the new day and new service
    C. Soul is home with the Lord

Part 4

Questions People Ask

For now we see through a glass, darkly; but then
face to face: now I know in part; but then shall
I know even as also I am known.

(1 Corinthians 13:12)

If any of you lack wisdom, let him ask of God, that
giveth to all men liberally, and upbraideth not; and
it shall be given him.

(James 1:5)

Casting all your care upon him; for he careth for you.

(1 Peter 5:7)

22

Questions Pastors Ask

1. The different stages in bereavement sound logical and right, but is there any biblical basis for them?

Since the Bible is not a book of psychology, we are not likely to find in it a discussion of the stages of bereavement. But we know of nothing in Scripture that contradicts what the psychologists have concluded concerning bereavement. Please keep in mind that not every person has the same kind of bereavement experience, and we must be careful not to force people's emotions into preconceived categories. Broken hearts do have to heal, and that is the general way in which they heal.

There is an interesting parallel between the stages of bereavement and the experience of Jeremiah as recorded in Lamentations. The book reveals the prophet's grief over the fall of Jerusalem. Note in chapter 1: his tears (v. 2), his unrest (v. 3), the bitterness within (v. 4), remembering (v. 7), and the feeling that his sorrow is greater than any other sorrow (v. 12). He expresses heartache (v. 20) and loneliness—there is nobody to comfort him (v. 2, 9, 17, 21).

The fact that Jeremiah expressed these deep emotions in an inspired book of the Bible would indicate that God expects us to grieve, and that He accepts our expressions of grief.

2. Should we just wait, then, for people to get over their grief?

No, we must assist them in the healing process. Time does not heal anything, because time is neutral. It is what we do with time that counts.

There is a great danger that the pastor get a mechanical model of this healing process rather than a dynamic model. When somebody loses a loved one, it is not like a machine losing a part which someday can be replaced or repaired. It is more like the amputation of a part of the living body, and that takes time to heal. There are adjustments to make, and most people can make them successfully if given enough encouragement and time.

For example, if a person loses his hearing, he is not likely to get it back again. He must face that fact honestly and start making adjustments. His hearing can never be exactly what it was before.

When a person loses a loved one, that relationship is broken and can never be repaired in this life. He must make adjustments and learn to live with the new situation. He cannot do that alone: he needs the encouragement of compassionate friends and the enablement God can give by His Spirit.

3. Funerals take up so much time! How can I be more efficient and still do my best?

Most important is the pastor's personal walk with the Lord. If we are abiding in Christ, He will provide the wisdom, strength, and ministry that we need.

Cultivate what Andrew Blackwood called "the sermonic seed plot." It is not at all macabre for the pastor to be thinking about what he would say if certain people in the church should be called home. (He would certainly be unwise to tell these people that he is preparing their funeral message!) We have had the experience of receiving the right message just hours before the funeral service. But that would not have happened had we not been meditating and studying the Word well in advance. Seeds we plant in our hearts months before can suddenly bear fruit.

We have also discovered that God speaks to us as we minister to His people in love. In the home and at the time of visitation in the funeral home, the minister absorbs data that can assist him in preparing the service. "I being in the way, the Lord led me."

The pastor must always be working ahead in his ministry so that interruptions will not wreck his schedule and hinder his regular ministry. The pastoral workaholic who has scheduled every hour of the day and every day of the week will see his beautiful edifice crumble with the announcement of a death in the church. Keep margins to your life and be flexible, and you will have an easier time handling the special demands that are bound to arise.

4. I belong to a fellowship that is strong on soul-winning and calling for a decision. You suggest that we "play down" such things as invitations and preaching about judgment.

We are not suggesting that any pastor "play down" the gospel or the truth of the Bible. We believe that each man must be true to his own gift and must fit into his own cultural situation. If it is a normal thing in your area for the minister to give an invitation at a funeral, then you certainly can do so without offending anybody. But in many parts of God's vineyard, invitations at funerals would create problems and be greatly misunderstood.

It is our conviction that the major purpose for the funeral is to minister comfort and help to the bereaved. If some of them are lost, then our goal is to win them to Christ; but we must be careful how we do it. The pastor who said, "Preaching to lost sinners at a funeral is like shooting fish in a barrel!" needed to be reminded that Bible fishermen used either a hook or a net, not a rifle. Nobody, including the lost sinner, likes to be cornered and exploited, especially at a funeral. In our zeal to win him, we may lose him and only deepen his prejudices against the gospel.

To be sure, there are exceptions. A high school Christian athlete died and left behind a winning testimony at school. It was only fitting that his funeral service include that witness. The pastor gave a public invitation for his school friends to accept Christ, and several responded. But the pastor was the father of the deceased boy, and he handled the service with tremendous love and grace. The people in the congregation, including the students, knew him and loved him. It was a special situation.

The harvest is not the end of the meeting; it is the end of the age. There is usually time and opportunity after the funeral to do personal work and seek to lead people to Christ. However, each minister must use his own gifts and follow the leading of the Spirit.

5. If the deceased person was a no-good wicked sinner, why not just say so?

When a person is "a no-good wicked sinner," nobody has to say much about it, because everybody already knows it. But why dwell on it? Jesus did not name the sins of the publicans, but He certainly exposed the sins of the self-righteous Pharisees. (compare Luke 15 with Matthew 23). He never called a single "wicked sinner" a "child of the devil," but He used that phrase when speaking to the religious Pharisees.

All we are suggesting is this: try not to magnify one kind of sin over another. There are Prodigal Sons and there are Elder Brothers. Focus on Jesus Christ and the forgiveness that God gives. Leave the examination and judgment to the Lord.

6. How can I "get a crowd" at funerals? Sometimes it's just the funeral director, a few friends, and myself.

People are busy these days, and often they pay their respects at the wake so they will not have to attend the funeral. Sometimes it is even difficult to gather enough men to be pallbearers.

Our people need to be taught the ministry of caring. If you have care groups in your church family, then assisting you in your funeral ministry can become a part of their caring. When we have had the funeral of an unchurched stranger, we have asked some of our retired people to assist and help build the crowd. Of course, the few friends and family who are there know that these people are imported, but they appreciate their help nonetheless.

7. I really can't stand the canned music they play in some funeral homes. What should I do?

There is probably very little you can do, if that is the kind of music the family has requested. If there is to be no soloist at the service, then why should the funeral director add to the family's bill by bringing in an organist? If you have an organist in your church who is willing to donate his or her talents, and if the funeral director agrees, then you have solved the problem.

People today are accustomed to canned music. They hear it in supermarkets, elevators, and even doctor's offices. Perhaps you are more sensitive to it than the funeral congregation is, since you minister week by week in an atmosphere of live music. Be patient and kind.

8. What kind of funeral records should I keep?

The law requires each pastor and church to keep records of funeral services, and special books (or file forms) are available. The pastor will certainly want to keep a record of each service so that he will not find himself duplicating messages. This record will also assist him in remembering with his people the anniversaries of the homegoing of loved ones. Both the pastor and the church should have records so that, should the pastor change churches, he will not walk off with the files.

Many funeral directors give the pastor an official record of the funeral service with pertinent data about the deceased and the family. This can easily be copied and given to the church clerk.

9. I'm always nervous about *starting* a funeral service. Sometimes people are talking or moving around. How do I get their attention?

We have been grateful to the funeral directors who have assisted us in this matter. When the service is about to start, the funeral director walks up to the lectern and turns on the light. As soon as he leaves, we like to walk *up to the casket* (even if it is closed) and stand there with bowed head, praying for God's help for ourselves and His people. Usually, by the time we step to the lecturn to open the service, the people have come to attention.

In the church or church chapel, of course, the entrance of the pastor should signal silence. In some funeral homes, the family enters and is seated before the pastor comes in, and this helps to signal silence and attention.

It is best for the pastor not to try to seat people or quiet them down. Most funeral directors are experienced in this and can get the congregation ready for the ministry of the Word. Sometimes there are people present who may have little culture or manners, and we must not be too hard on them.

10. What do you do with babies at funeral services?

Endure them.

We have never been able to understand why people bring little babies to funerals. Surely, when there is a death in a family or neighborhood, friends are only too happy to step in and help. But, like the poor, babies at funerals will always be with us.

If the funeral is to be at the church, perhaps some of the members would open the nursery and make its services available. This would be especially helpful if you expect a large crowd.

At the funeral home, it's a different matter; and you had better let the funeral director solve the problem. He can see to it that mothers with babies can sit near an exit, or at least on an aisle. We recall one service where the secretary of the funeral home offered to help and kept the infant in the office until the service was ended. Bless her!

11. Should the men wear their hats at the cemetery during the committal service?

Not unless the weather is bad. If so, it is perfectly permissible for the men to keep their hats on, even during prayer.

(They did it during Spurgeon's committal service.) The best way to show respect to the dead is to be thoughtful and kind to the living.

If the committal service is held at a cemetery chapel, away from the grave, then obviously the men should remove their hats.

The funeral director can let the pallbearers know that it is all right for them to keep their hats on, and they can perhaps spread the word to others. Before the pastor begins the graveside service, it would be in order for the funeral director to say, "Gentlemen, it is in order to keep your hats on during this brief service."

And if the weather is cold and uncomfortable, *keep the service brief.*

23

Questions Mourners Ask

1. Is our deceased child now an angel?

No believer who dies, adult or child, ever becomes an angel. God's glorified children are much higher than the angels. The idea that the dead become angels comes from a misinterpretation of Matthew 22:30. God's resurrected people are like the angels in only one thing: they will not marry or be given in marriage. But they do not become angels.

2. Will our deceased child remain a child?

The Bible does not give us a great deal of information about the future state or the intermediate state between death and resurrection. Since heaven is a place of perfection, it would appear that babies and little children mature so that they can enjoy heaven and worship and serve God. It would seem out of place for helpless infants to be inhabiting heaven, especially when you consider how many babies have died over the centuries.

We know that God will do what is best. Certainly parents will know their children (1 Cor. 13:12) and children their parents, and there will be perfect joy and fellowship.

3. Do our loved ones in heaven know what we're doing on earth?

There is no clear evidence that they do. Luke 15:7 and 10 teach that there is joy in heaven when a sinner is saved, so perhaps loved ones in heaven "get the message" when someone they knew and loved has trusted Christ. Hebrews 12:1 is sometimes used to prove that saints in heaven watch the church on earth, but the word *witnesses* does not necessarily mean *spectators*. It relates to chapter 11 where God bore witness to the great men and women of faith, and they, by their lives and deaths, bear witness to us. The "cloud of witnesses" is not watching us; rather, we watch them as we read the Scriptures and see how God honored their faith.

Our loving Father in heaven will see to it that all of His children will be happy and content. If He feels they need to know something about what's going on below, He will give them that information. It is our feeling that the glories of heaven will so captivate the saints above that they will not take much interest in things on earth, except, of course, the conversion of sinners.

4. How can we show our love for a deceased person?

By showing love to those who are left behind. We must be very careful not to get involved in some kind of mystical relationship with the dead, lest Satan get a foothold and create problems. Since God's church militant and God's church triumphant worship the same God and Savior, there is a spiritual relationship of some kind. The last verse of "The Church's One Foundation" expresses it this way:

> Yet she on earth hath union
> With God the Three in One,
> And mystic sweet communion
> With those whose rest is won.
> (Samuel J. Stone)

We are not sure what this "mystic sweet communion" is, and it is best we not try to cultivate it. The best way to show love for the dead is to remember them with gratitude and seek to serve others in love while we and they are still alive.

5. I know my loved one is in heaven, but I keep thinking about her body in that cold ground. How can I get over this?

We know our loved ones because of *physical* appearance and experiences, so it's not unusual that we get attached to the body the person inhabited. If we have cared for the dead body properly, honored the person, and given Christian burial, that is about all we can do. It is probably best to "set our attention on things above" and not brood over the physical.

If a person has an *abnormal* attachment to the physical, he or she may need special help. We have known people to weep because it was "raining on their loved ones," and so on, and this kind of reaction is, of course, a bit eccentric. One purpose of the funeral service is to give us opportunity to say good-bye to the remains and begin our detachment from that body, which is now dead. With some people it takes more time, and we must be patient.

6. Will we recognize our loved ones in heaven?

Yes (1 Cor. 13:12). Peter, James, and John recognized Moses and Elijah in glory, and yet these men had never met (Matt. 17:1-4). As one pastor said, "Certainly we won't be less intelligent in heaven than we are here!"

7. When I visit the grave, is it OK for me to talk to my loved one?

Many people do this in a sentimental way, and if it stays on that level, it is a harmless practice. We know that we are really talking to ourselves, and that may not hurt. Some bereaved people have worked out their inner hurts and perplexities this way. They would probably accomplish just as much if they talked frankly with a pastor or close friend.

It is when a harmless sentimental practice becomes a habit or an obsession that there is danger. And talking to the dead could give our enemy opportunity to move in with a demonic counterfeit. It is best to talk to the living God and His living people.

8. I didn't follow my loved one's wishes exactly when it came to the funeral, and now I feel guilty. What should I do?

This is not an unusual problem. For example, a loved one may have wanted to be cremated, and the family decided not to. Or the family may determine to bury the body in a different cemetery.

To begin with, we must learn to accept the past because it cannot be changed. What can be changed is our interpretation and application of the past. It is not going to ruin some great eternal plan if we did not fulfill every desire of the deceased loved one. Some decisions we make have to be happy compromises, and such compromises are not evil. After all, the burial of a loved one is a *family* affair, and more than one opinion must be considered.

If you feel you have really sinned, then confess it to the Lord and ask His cleansing (1 John 1:9; Psalm 51). However, if what you did is not really sin, face it for what it really is: the normal guilt feelings that often accompany bereavement. Admit them, learn to smile at them, and remind yourself that you did your best. Obsessive guilt can become a serious problem in the life of a bereaved person, and we must beware.

9. How long will it take me to get over this?

It all depends on how you adjust to reality and learn to accept life in God's will. It usually takes several months for the "deep grief" to pass so that you are able to talk about the loved one, and even smile or laugh, and not feel hurt or guilty. When you can talk openly about the loved one realistically, you are well on your way to healing.

Be kind to yourself and patient. Beware of nursing your grief in an abnormal way, because that only delays healing. People will sympathize with you for only so long; then they will expect you to return to life with its burdens and battles. Your grief must not become a crutch on which you lean, either to get sympathy or to avoid responsibility.

In former days, society set a definite limit to the period of mourning. We do not not have such limits today, but perhaps we should. At any rate, once the deep hurt starts to heal (and it may never *completely* heal), you are on your way. God can heal the brokenhearted if we give Him all the pieces.

10. Do I dare ever attend another funeral?

Of course. To begin with, mourning with others is good for you. A broken heart does not heal by being isolated from reality. It heals by facing reality and depending on the grace of God. Don't be afraid to weep. People know what you have been through. If you don't want to attend, don't force yourself; but at the same time, don't pamper yourself.

11. How should I act when I first return to church?

Act like a person who has just come through the valley and is on the way to victory. Let the pastor know when you will be coming back. He may want to say something publicly and also include you and your loved ones in the pastoral prayer. Of course, people will greet you and some of them may say the wrong thing; but love them just the same.

One of the best places to get healing is in the fellowship of God's loving people. It will take time to adjust to new relationships in the church, but that will come with time. Trust God—and trust God's people.

12. What shall I do when I dream about my deceased loved one?

It is not unusual for us to dream about the dead. After all, we can't control our dreams, but we can control how we respond to them. Don't take your dreams too seriously. Dreaming about your loved one can help you adjust to reality. However, beware of taking orders from people you see in your dreams. You are not obligated to do what they tell you. In past ages,

God did communicate with people through dreams; but today He communicates through His Word.

We may have dreams about our deceased loved ones until the Lord calls us home. There is no way to predict these things. Just don't treat your dreams as divine communications.

An Informal
Bibliography

The following books have been a help to us. We do not necessarily agree with everything in them, but we have learned from them. The inclusion of a title in this bibliography is not an endorsement of everything the author has written, preached, or taught. Some of these titles may be out of print, but they are worth searching for.

GOING THROUGH THE VALLEY
Many people have written about their experiences of grief, and these autobiographical personal testimonies can be very helpful to those who seek to comfort the sorrowing.

One of the best is *The Last Thing We Talk About*, by Joseph Bayly (Elgin, Ill.: David C. Cook, 1973). *A Grief Observed*, by C. S. Lewis (New York: Seabury, 1963), records his reactions after the death of his wife. *Not by Accident*, by Isabel Fleece (Chicago: Moody, 1964), tells how Dr. and Mrs. Fleece responded to the accidental death of a son. *A Letter of Consolation* is Henri J. M. Nouwen's reflections on the death of his mother (New York: Harper & Row, 1982). *But for Our Grief*, by June Taylor (New York: Holman, 1977), is a mother's account of the death of a daughter and how she and the family found comfort. *When Death Takes a Father* (Grand Rapids: Baker, Direction, 1974) is Gladys Kooiman's personal account of her own pilgrimage through the valley when her husband died. *William's Story*, by Rosemary Attlee (Wheaton: Harold Shaw, 1983), is a mother's story of her son's battle against cancer. Read it in conjunction with John Gunther's *Death Be Not Proud* (New York: Harper & Row, 1949). *Adventure in Dying* (Chicago: Moody, 1976), by Nancy Karo (with Alvera Mickelson), tells the story of a young pastor's death and how the "adventure" affected his home and church. *Fear No Evil* (Wheaton, Ill.: Harold Shaw, 1984) is by the late David Watson and tells of his one-year bout with cancer and what God did for him and his church.

THE THEOLOGY OF DEATH

The Christian Way of Death, by Gladys Hunt (Grand Rapids: Zondervan, 1971), is one evangelical Christian's reply to the popular *The American Way of Death*, by Jessica Mitford (New York: Simon & Schuster, 1963). It is brief, biblical, practical, and tender. *Perspectives on Death*, edited by Liston O. Mills (Nashville: Abingdon, 1969), is an anthology of nine excellent essays on various aspects of death, from the biblical viewpoint as well as various academic disciplines. In *Living with Death*, the popular German theologian-preacher Helmut Thielicke wrestles with theological and philosophical problems (Grand Rapids: Eerdmans, 1983). *The Other Side of Life*, by Rusty Wright (San Bernadino, Calif.: Here's Life, 1979), is a popular treatment of the biblical doctrine of death, with a good chapter on out-of-body experiences. Loraine Boettner's *Immortality* is a classic work on the future life (Nutley, N.J.: Presb. & Ref., 1956). Two treatments of death and resurrection in a popular approach are *Life in the Afterlife*, by Tim LaHaye (Wheaton, Ill.: Tyndale, 1980), and *The Other Side of Death*, by Tal Brooke (Wheaton: Tyndale, 1979). *Heaven*, by Charles Ferguson Ball (Wheaton: Scripture Press, Victor, 1980), gives biblical answers to most questions people ask about the future life. *The Last Enemy*, by Richard Wolf (Washington, D.C.: Canon, 1974), is a satisfying discussion of what the Bible teaches about death. It contains brief surveys of Eastern and Western traditions and funeral customs, and also a chapter on suicide.

DEATH AND MODERN MAN

Much is being written these days by psychologists, sociologists, and philosophers on the subject of death and dying.

Death and Western Thought, by Jacques Choron (New York: Collier, 1963), gives an excellent survey of what philosophers have believed and taught about death over the centuries. A fine overview. *Western Attitudes Toward Death*, by Philippe Aries (Baltimore: Johns Hopkins U., 1975), covers the subject from the Middle Ages to the present, documenting changing attitudes as shown in religion and literature. *Death, the Final Frontier* by Dale V. Hardt (Englewood Cliffs, N.J.: Prentice-Hall, 1979), is one of the best surveys you will find, dealing with cultural, scientific, legal, and religious aspects of death. There is an excellent chapter on cremation. *Overcoming the Fear of Death*, by David Cole Gordon (reprint; New York: Penguin Books, Pelican, 1972), is a humanistic approach to the subject that will help you better understand what the man on the street is thinking—or *wants* to think!

FUNERALS

Jessica Mitford's *The American Way of Death* (New York; Simon and Schuster, 1963) is the classic attack on the funeral industry. *The High Cost of Dying*, by Ruth Mulvey Harmer (New York: Collier Books, 1963), covers the same ground. Both books promote memorial associations and condemn most modern funeral practices. Take both books with a grain or two of salt.

The best general book for pastors is *The Funeral*, by Andrew W. Blackwood (Philadelphia: Westminster, 1942; also available in a Baker Book House reprint). We confess our indebtedness to Dr. Blackwood for our own views of funeral ministry. *The Funeral: Vestige or Value?* by Paul E. Irion (Nashville: Abingdon, 1966), discusses the changing patterns of modern funerals and offers some excellent insights for the Christian minister. His book *The Funeral and the Mourners* (Nashville: Abingdon, 1954) stands next to Blackwood's text as a practical guide for pastoral care of the bereaved. His philosophy of the funeral is excellent.

THE GRIEF PROCESS

The classic text is *Good Grief*, by Granger E. Westberg (Philadelphia: Fortress, 1962). You ought to have extra copies to share with sorrowing people. *Grief's Healing Process*, by Charles M. Sell (Portland, Ore.: Multnomah, 1984), is a small booklet that contains a wealth of helpful material. Again, have copies available to give to others. *Grief*, by Haddon W. Robinson (Grand Rapids: Zondervan, 1974), is a beautiful booklet that can be shared with grieving people. It was originally published for the Christian Medical Society. *Understanding Grief* and *The Many Faces of Grief*, both by Edgar Jackson (Nashville: Abingdon, 1957 and 1977), are sensitive and practical studies of the grief process.

The name of Elisabeth Kubler-Ross has long been associated with studies in death and dying. *On Death and Dying* is one of her classic texts (New York: Macmillan, 1969). *Death: The Final Stage in Growth* (Englewood Cliffs, N.J.: Prentice-Hall, 1975) is a collection of essays relating to the subject. You will not find much Christian theology here, but some of the chapters are insightful. *On Children and Death* (New York: Macmillan, 1983) contains some poignant material and some useful insights, but it is far too sentimental and mystical for the Christian minister. *The Bereaved Parent*, by Harriet Sarnoff Schiff (New York: Penguin, 1978), gives some excellent help to the family that has lost a child. *Helping Children Cope with Death*, by Robert V. Dodd (Scottsdale, Pa.: Herald, 1984), is a pastoral approach with a biblical emphasis. The booklet is not expensive and should be made available to those who work with children who have lost a parent. Another helpful Herald Press book is *Learning to Die*, by Samuel Gerber (1984). One of the best booklets to put into the hands of the dying is *You Can Live Without Fear of Death*, by Richard A. Bodey (Grand Rapids: Baker, 1980). It has a clear gospel message presented in a warm pastoral manner. *Living with Loss*, by Ronald W. Ramsay and Rene Noorbergen (New York: William Morrow, 1981), presents the confrontation approach to grief therapy.

SUICIDE

The Savage God, by A. Alvarez (New York: Random House, 1972), is written by a professional writer who once attempted suicide. He focuses on literary figures, such as Sylvia Plath, and draws very few practical conclusions that a Christian minister could apply. But the book has become a classic and should be read. University students are reading it. Karl Menninger's *Man Against Himself* is the basic text on suicide from the psychiatric point of view (New York: Harcourt Brace, 1938, 1956). *Suicide in America*, by Herbert Hendin (New York: Norton,

1982), contains a great deal of psychological and statistical material on the subject. A valuable text. *Suicide and Grief*, by Howard W. Stone (Philadelphia: Fortress, 1972), explains the dynamics of the grief process when a loved one commits suicide. A good book for the pastor to study. *English Debate on Suicide from Donne to Hume*, by S. E. Sprott (LaSalle, Ill.: Open Court, 1961), presents historical data on the debate over whether or not people have the right to commit suicide. It is a fascinating study that shows the influence of wrong thinking on human decisions. *Understanding Suicide*, by William L. Coleman (Elgin, Ill.: David C. Cook, 1979), is a compassionate evangelical survey of the subject, a helpful guide for all who deal with potential suicides or their grieving families. *The Urge to Die*, by Peter Giovacchini (New York: Macmillan, 1981), is a psychological study of why young people commit suicide. Two other helpful books on suicide are: *After Suicide*, by John H. Hewett (Philadelphia: Westminster, 1980), and *What You Should Know About Suicide*, by Bill Blackburn (Waco, Tex.: Word, 1982).

THE PROBLEM OF EVIL IN THE WORLD

The Problem of Pain, by C. S. Lewis, is the classic text (London: Geoffrey Bles, 1940; New York: Macmillan, 1944). *Where Is God When It Hurts?* edited by Philip Yancey (Grand Rapids: Zondervan, 1977), is a popular treatment with good examples of people turning trial into triumph. *In God's Waiting Room*, by Dr. Lehman Strauss (Chicago: Moody, 1985), is a beautiful treatment of suffering by a Bible scholar who experienced trials personally. An excellent book to share with those who suffer. *The Mystery of Suffering*, by Hugh Evan Hopkins (Chicago: InterVarsity, 1959), is a good survey of biblical teaching about suffering, as is *The Paradox of Pain*, by A. E. Wilder Smith (Wheaton: Harold Shaw, 1971). *Why Us?* by Warren W. Wiersbe (Old Tappan, N.J.: Revel, 1983), presents a biblical view of suffering in answer to Harold Kushner's *When Bad Things Happen to Good People* (New York: Schocken; 1981). *Suffering*, by Erhard S. Gerstenberger and Wolfgang Schrage (Nashville: Abingdon, 1980), is a fine survey of the biblical data on human suffering.

OTHER HELPFUL BOOKS

The Jewish Way in Death and Mourning, by Maurice Lamm (New York: Jonathan David, 1969), presents the orthodox Jewish view of death, mourning, and the funeral. Interesting and helpful even to non-Jewish readers. *The Oxford Book of Death*, compiled and edited by D. J. Enright (New York: Oxford U., 1983), is a fascinating anthology of material dealing with various aspects of death. The material is very quotable. *Consolation*, compiled by Mrs. Charles E. Cowman (Los Angeles: Cowman Publications, 1944; Grand Rapids: Zondervan, 1945), is a superior anthology of Christian thinking about death and sorrow. Very helpful for planning funeral messages. Two other useful anthologies are: *A Treasury of Comfort*, edited by Sidney Greenberg (New York: Crown, 1954; New York: Hartmore, 1967), and *In the Midst of Winter*, edited by Mary Jane Moffatt (New York: Random House,1982).

Moody Press, a ministry of the Moody Bible Institute, is designed for education, evangelization, and edification. If we may assist you in knowing more about Christ and the Christian life, please write us without obligation: Moody Press, c/o MLM, Chicago, IL 60610.